I Sit Listening to the Wind

Reviews of *I SIT LISTENING TO THE WIND*

An invitation to the magic inner circle . . .

"Written with sound Jungian psychology and gentle intuitiveness, yet stirred by assertiveness, Duerk invites us into that magic inner circle of the Feminine Mystique, urging us to use the Masculine energy productively and wisely. Highly recommended."—*Spiritual Studies Center Booknews*

An encouragement to be inwardly reflective . . .

"A nourishing, tenderly understanding, helpful book about the Masculine within women that encourages readers to be inwardly attentive and reflective."—Jean Shinoda Bolen, M.D., Author of *Goddesses in Everywoman* and *Crossing to Avalon*

Harmony to live by . . .

"In contrast to feminists who talk about rights to fight for, Judith Duerk talks about harmony to live by. *I Sit Listening to the Wind* speaks of a different way for the next generation, the daughters of the women who give voice to their experiences in Judith's book."—Edith Wallace, M.D., Ph.D., Jungian Analyst; Author of *A Queen's Quest: Pilgrimage for Individuation*

Gently powerful and healing . . .

"Again, Judith Duerk shows us that there is a path of our own that we can follow to find a way of encountering the Masculine side of ourselves. The intimacy of the imagery and the feminine quality of her presentation makes her writing unique . . . gently powerful . . . healing."—Kay Bradway, Ph.D., Founding Member of the C.G. Jung Institute of San Francisco; Author of *Villa of Mysteries* and Co-author of *Sandplay: Silent Workshop of the Psyche*

A book you'll read again and again . . .

"Written in [a] meditative mixture of prose, poetry, and reflective questions . . . this is a quiet, passionate book you'll be reading again and again."—*Chinaberry Catalog*

Auditory training for the soul . . .

"*I Sit Listening to the Wind* attunes a third ear to hear faint musings of awareness, screeches of outrage, tears of loss, and gleanings of wisdom. Duerk coaxes them into consciousness with respect for the Feminine experience. Auditory training for the soul."—Christella Carbaugh, SLW, Coordinator of Spiritual Life, Sisters of the Living Work

An essential book for women . . .

"Judith models the best of Feminine Persuasion, a meditative invitation for the reader to attune to the Deepest Authority: HerSelf."—Christina Baldwin, Author of *Calling the Circle: The First and Future Culture* and Co-founder of Peer Spirit Circling

A primer for becoming fully yourself . . .

"A valuable primer for a woman seeking to become fully herself. Step by step Judith Duerk leads us through the struggle to realize a balanced life, as we vie with those two great forces, the Feminine and the Masculine. Using the voices of many women, she draws us into real life experience. In the company of these women, we find a mirror for the passage we call our own."—Betty De Shong Meador, Ph.D., Jungian Analyst; Author of *Uncursing the Dark*

A call to take time to listen . . .

"How many times in the busyness of our lives do we take time to listen to the wind? This book is the reflection of one woman who took time to be with herself and discovered a new source of time—Kairos . . . sacred time."—*Crone Chronicles*

CIRCLE OF STONE SERIES

BY JUDITH DUERK

Volume 1
CIRCLE OF STONES
Woman's Journey To Herself

Volume II
I SIT LISTENING TO THE WIND
Woman's Encounter Within Herself

New Revised Edition

I Sit Listening to the Wind

Woman's Encounter Within Herself

By Judith Duerk

Innisfree Press, Inc.

Innisfree Press, Inc.
136 Roumfort Road
Philadelphia, PA 19119-1632
Vist our Web site at www.InnisfreePress.com

Library of Congress Cataloging-in-Publication Data
Duerk, Judith.
Circle of stones / by Judith Duerk.
p.   cm. — (Circle of stones series ; v. 1-2)
Originally published: San Diego, Calif. : LuraMedia, 1989-1993
Contents: v. 1. Woman's journey to herself —
v. 2. I sit listening to the wind : woman's encounter within herself.
ISBN 1-880913-36-4 (v. 1 : pb). — ISBN 1-880913037-2 (v. 2 : pb)
1. Women—Psychology. 2. Women—Identity. 3. Femininity.
4. Identity (Psychology). 5. Sex role.
I. Duerk, Judith. I sit listening to the wind. II. Title.
III. Series: Duerk, Judith. Circle of stones series : v. 1-2.
HQ1206.D84   1999
155.3'33—dc21   98-52771

Innisfree
Press, Inc.

A call to the
deep heart's core

Acknowledgements

My thanks to the women who have allowed the use of their dreams and writings and to the circles of women everywhere who have given loving encouragement as this book progressed.

My acknowledgment to LuraMedia (the original publisher) and to the courage and risk-taking of Lura Geiger in dealing with a complex and difficult subject. And to Marcia Broucek at Innisfree Press for her vision and dedication in publishing this new edition.

My gratitude to Bobbi Kadesh for her help in preparing the manuscript and for her good humour and patience in all stages of the work.

And lastly, my heartfelt appreciation to my husband, my two sons, and my brother for support during the entire effort. This writing could not have been brought to completion without the real and honest support from both the Feminine and Masculine realms.

to

the memory

of a woman

who struggled

to

bring forth

herself

Contents

How might your life have been different if, once, as a young girl, you had wandered alone in the woodlands not far from your mother's home . . . and you had come upon a small glade you had never seen before?

If you had listened to the wind blow mysteriously . . . had seen, there in the shadows, a group of rough-hewn stones, gathered in a circle . . . and, somehow, you knew that this was a place where women gathered throughout the ages to reflect upon their lives?

And, if, as you sat down on one of the stones, you could feel the presence of those women reaching out to welcome you . . .

How might your life be different?

Preface

I sit listening, the wind blows . . . An image comes to me . . . of a woman in a moment of reflection, sitting quietly to listen within. She listens to her own Feminine feelings and perceptions, but also to her inner Masculine side, in wonder at its energy and what it stirs within her. Sensing, with an ancient sense, the work that is hers to do to develop herself and her gifts . . . seeking to hold her ground and not be blown away.

Then, in her own individual way, she enters a life-long encounter as she engages with this Masculine energy, which spiritual traditions throughout the ages have characterized as "the Wind." It is the Masculine/Yang energy within a woman's Feminine/Yin psyche: the small Yang circle of light within her soft Yin darkness. It brings her balance and strength and completes her wholeness as a woman.

Jung called this Masculine energy the "animus."

I think of the great cycles of a woman's life, of early bonding with the mother . . . through that bond, a grounding in the Archetypal Feminine . . . underneath that, roots in the deeper Self. Then the awakening of her Masculine side and a loosening of those earlier bonds . . . as she fulfills her achievement side, schooling and professional life . . . perhaps marriage and children. Years of fulfilling her obligations in the collective realm.

For modern woman there follows a period of great possibility, of consciously seeking the help of her animus to focus on Feminine values and bring them to form in her life. And in later years, the journey back to Feminine ground . . . her devotion in that realm, as she brings forth her truest voice.

In a complete absence of animus energy, there is no life, the air is dead. A woman is unable to develop, remains without clarity or focus. But for many modern women, that Masculine energy is ever there, ever blowing, filling any vacuum left when she fails to know her feelings or define her values . . . filling the void with judgements and criticisms repeated from the society around her, with little regard for the woman's own subjective truth or wisdom.

The woman must form a relationship with this Masculine side of herself or it will operate autonomously, convincing her that she is always so right that she may not be able to see that she is out of control. Until she forms this relationship, her own womanly energy will be spent in service to the collective realm. And her woman life is lost!

The following story illustrates a modern woman's dilemma:

> *Already a physician in Europe, a woman had earned two doctoral degrees in America before returning abroad for training as a psychoanalyst. Early in that work, she remarked to her professor, a man of compassion and honesty, that she feared she might have too much ego to submit willingly to the work. His reply was that she had "very little Feminine ego at all, only a highly trained animus."*

Thus begins the story of modern woman's encounter within.

❖ ❖ ❖

The years spent working with this material have been difficult. Even as I write these words, I am aware of a voice: "This book is neither definitive nor authoritative. It is too subjective to be of consequence. Mostly," says the voice, "everyone knows all of this already.

"And besides, it's a trifle boring!"

I smile. How like that voice within a woman, as it dismisses her, to end with a little swipe: "and haven't you put on a bit of weight?"

This writing was begun to explore the dismissing voices of the Masculine side of a woman as she struggles to listen within and to bring forth her own perceptions. *And, even as I write of the dismissing voices, a voice dismisses me.*

Writing of woman's Masculine side has been a very different experience from writing of the Feminine realm in *Circle of Stones*. My animus began with such wit and verve that it took me several chapters to realize that I had been tricked: He wanted to make this book a compendium about himself, quite unrelated to woman's life and needs.

An old idea says that speaking of an Archetype brings it to life right there in the room. And it proved disturbingly true! The animus did not want to be revealed as he really was, but capered around the room, distracting me in a dozen directions, or crept in, wordy and pompous, with grandiose proclamations. Strife erupted in our household between me and my husband, my sons. I remembered that the animus makes mischief between a woman and the men around her, but I wasn't quite prepared for this!

I knew that I must renew my grounding in the Feminine realm. I spent many days in the woods, simply picking up sticks . . . remembering how deeply I cared for the women for whom I was preparing this writing . . . how devoted I felt to the Feminine process of us all.

I could feel the pathos of women today with our highly developed animus, confronted with the eternal paradox: The nature of the Yin is receptive, to yield; the nature of the Yang is to dominate. The two are forever equal and necessary to the fulfillment of the cosmic cycle. We modern women, with our powerfully developed inner Masculine side, are faced with a new dilemma: whether to ground ourselves in the vibrant receptivity of the Yin, or to give over to our dynamic and compelling animus mode.

If a woman lacks the steadfastness and self-restraint required to remain centered in the Yin, she may abdicate completely to an animus mode. She loses her footing in the Feminine ground, and her connection through it to the deeper Self, and accommodates to a group ethos.

There is a broader pattern in our country similar to this, in which both men and women go to extreme measures to accommodate to the group, leaving behind their individual connection to the deeper Self. Surely this pattern needs to be broken, particularly in these critical times when the deepest possible wisdom is called for!

Perhaps modern woman has no idea how profoundly she is needed. The world is crying out for a developed Feminine voice, a voice that can mediate, once again, the ancient values of the Feminine: values of interiority and of the sacredness of matter, values that honour the privacy of individual process . . . the values of the deeper Self held within us all.

In her efforts to effect change in our society, woman today may not realize that she leaves unexplored Feminine modes that might accomplish the same ends if she could rediscover them . . . modes of holding within herself her vision of what could be, of gestating that vision with a spiritual energy that is uniquely Feminine, and finally bringing it forth in a circumspect womanly voice.

There is a story of canaries, valued for their sensitivities, taken below the surface in old mines to test for poison gas. We women, today, frequently express impatience with ourselves for being "overly sensitive." Yet, I sense that our culture is in desperate need of women of sensitivity and courage who can point out what is poisonous just below the surface . . . women who have grounded themselves, developed their vision and voice, and can identify what is twisted in our society today.

In my writing, I speak often of daughters, but I do not mean biological daughters. I am fiercely proud of my sons and of their spiritual energy. Yet, I recognize a distinctly Feminine spiritual energy, an energy that flows from the Archetypal Great Mother herself. I ask myself how we women today can open ourselves to this ancient flow . . . let it flow through us to our daughters, to the women of the future, to the daughters of all of us.

An ancient Oriental image reveals beautifully the relationship of the mature woman with her developed animus: It is the lingam in the yoni, the phallus embraced in the vulva. The image symbolizes the Masculine energy within a woman's psyche offering itself in devotion and loving penetration . . . Offering its energy in willing commitment to the woman, as she, with her roots in the ground of the Yin, brings forth the flowering of the Feminine Self.

I offer this book not as an encyclopedia about the animus, but as a helpful companion to sustain a woman as she begins her encounter within.

Her Grounding

In The Feminine

A sense of time

> I sit listening to the wind . . .
>> . . . the woods are cool and quiet.

The wind blows . . . brings a memory from many years ago:

> *The storms of early autumn had felled large trees and branches in the woods nearby. For several days the men had worked to clear away the timber. The firewood had been cut in lengths and neatly stacked to dry. What was left was in a heap of tangled brush and twigs. It was an eyesore, in the way, and in the very place I had wanted to write for the next few days.*

> *There was no one else to clean it up, so I started with a vengeance, intending to make short shrift of it and get on with my real work. For a few hours I laboured furiously, pulling at the pile, grabbing at the ends of the largest branches, trying to disentangle the heap by sheer brute force and my accumulated animosity. I learned later that a young woodsman had returned, willing to work, but had fled in fright before the ferocity of my face and efforts.*

> *By late morning, it was clear that nothing effective was happening. My petulant tearings and rippings at the pile finally began to slow down. Much of my irritation had worn itself off . . . the woods had worked its way.*

> *I stopped to sit on a nearby rock and knew that I must eat.*

> *When I went back to work, it was with a different energy . . . no longer impatiently pulling at the protruding limbs or trying to overturn the heap. With clippers, I began to trim whatever*

offered itself from the stack. In my agitation of the morning, I had not seen that it could be approached in this way.

By late afternoon, I knew there was no way that the task would be finished that day. I began to work more slowly to sink into my experience with the brush. To the right went branches, neatly stacked, ready for drying or burning. To the left, I placed little bundles of twigs to be used later as kindling.

As the shadows lengthened, a quieter rhythm emerged. The task seemed more worthy of itself . . . my real work, less pressing. I stopped before I grew too tired and, much to my surprise, began to write, as I had first intended, right there beside the brush.

On the morning of the second day, I awakened early with a sense of eagerness, not to finish the job of clearing, but to see what the day might bring if I offered myself to the task. At intervals I rested, with no clear plan for what must be completed that day. It was almost no surprise to find myself writing in the woods as I rested.

The day passed.

Near the middle of the third day, I became aware of something wondrous happening. My whole experience was shifting . . . the molecules of time, itself, opened up before me, spreading themselves apart so that there was space and breadth amongst them . . . breath to breathe within each moment.

I laid down the clippers and sat on the rock to sense the moment more fully, as I had not allowed myself to do the day before.

I saw the wind in the tallest trees slowly stir the leaves. The colours shifted from darkest greens to black . . . to nearly yellow. A hush was in the woods around, as well as deep within, me. I watched there, while the sun set, then walked silently to the house.

A sense of time

I washed my hair and did the few things necessary to prepare for the coming week.

The next morning, as the fourth day dawned, the whole house lay in quietness. The preparations of the evening before, undertaken out of the silence, had emerged from a sense of ordering far deeper than conscious planning. What had not been done never would be missed.

When I returned to the woods to work, I carried a broom with the clippers. By noontime, all of the remaining twigs had been put into the little bundles and tied with yarn from the house, for there was no twine. I swept the ground where the brush had been, smoothing out the last bits of bark. The earth lay flat and clean again . . . the grass, a pale yellow.

The wind blows . . . I sit listening against a tree.

Many times, through the years, I have remembered that day. There was a sense of being deep within the doing. Rather than a driven way of pressing to complete the task, knowing every second what the next ten thousand would hold, it was as if I had slipped through a scrim into a timeless, mysterious realm . . . silent . . . shimmering with life.

One whole day of being, not in ordinary Chronos time, but in the sacred Kairos time of the Feminine realm. I had glimpsed a way of being in which time, itself, was sentient, quivering with its own awareness of what each moment could hold.

One moment, I had been trapped by time, cut off from myself. In the next moment, time itself was alive, connecting me to my feelings, to all things in the circle of life . . . to a way of being, from long ago when the earth was still held sacred. When a woman knew that her task was necessary to the cycles of nature. Knew that her devotion within, as she fulfilled the task, reconsecrated the earth and echoed throughout the cosmos.

I lean against the tree, thinking of our needs as women. Our ordinary lives are no longer lived in nature. It is difficult, in daily life, to find the Feminine realm. The drawing of the water, the gathering of the grains no longer are performed under an open sky. Even the machines that assist a woman prevent her from holding the elemental in her hands. The sense of her task as consecrated and necessary to the cosmos is gone.

And I fear for women yet to come. For under the pressures of modern life, time has become compressed. The Feminine sense of time has all but disappeared. Yet woman cannot exist with only a linear awareness of time, for her sense of sacred Kairos time is the precious essence of life. There must be time enough for her to experience the sacredness within each moment and within herself.

How can woman redeem what was lost so long ago? For millennia, as she was defined by man, woman developed herself in the prevailing Masculine image. But the heroic journey of the Masculine, so long clearly delineated, could not provide what was needed to complete the journey of the conscious and developed Feminine. It could not help woman return to her Archetypal roots or to the sacredness of her sense of Kairos time.

The locust tree at my back sways. I sit, trying to understand the shift in my experiencing of time. What had made time so alive? Yet, even as I try so purposefully to comprehend the shift, wondering, perhaps, if I might make it happen, the precious aliveness dies. It cannot be made to happen!

Finally I sit empty, waiting.

A sense of time

❖ ❖ ❖

A single shaft of blinding sunlight pierces through the leaves . . . onto the bundles of twigs lying at my feet . . . touches the pages of my writing. I hold my breath as a thousand tiny sprinkles of light fill the air above. It could not be *made* to happen. Yet it is happening once more!

Time is alive again!

I sit listening to the wind . . . and I wonder how to be willing to offer myself into each moment . . . into *this* moment, now. How to give over, humbly, to the sovereignty, to the utter autonomy this moment seems to ask. How to let myself and the moment slip through the mysterious scrim
     . . . from the purposeful and known
     . . . to the timeless.

The leaves fall
     . . Time drifts by.

How might your life have been different if, when you felt time pressing in on you, there were a place to go where you were allowed to simply be? If, as you sat down silently, there were a sense of the presence of other women breathing in the stillness . . . waiting quietly with you?

And if you watched the dappled shadows on the ground around you as the wind suddenly stilled . . . and you entered a new sense of time, of time stretching out before you?

And you knew that there would finally be time enough for you . . .

How might your life be different?

A sense of identity

I sit listening . . .
. . . the wind blows.

An old woman sits with me . . . watches as the aspen leaves flutter to the ground . . . speaks of a past struggle:

"We entered, all alone, into the unknown . . . with little to support or sustain us from a familiar realm. There was no way a woman could succeed but to give up parts of herself!

"I was one of the few women at the conservatory when it was announced that a master class would be given by a woman of great renown. There were stories of superb artistry, as well as imprisonment and narrow escape in the war. Her concert the evening before the class brought tumultuous applause.

"I wondered at her appearance the next morning, as she walked across the stage: she carried a brown leather satchel, worn-looking, with a frayed handle . . . settled her materials on a small table, rather than on the podium standing imposingly alongside. One could see her frailness. Yet her presence filled the concert hall in a way I had not seen before.

"She requested a glass of water and asked to be certain that those in the audience, waiting with impatience, were comfortable. The last thing she did, before she began to teach, was to cross over to where her brown satchel sat on the floor. She took out a faded, rose-coloured sweater, which she put on over her elegant gown. There was a small hole at the left elbow.

"She said the hall felt a little drafty.

"The audience, candidates for graduate degrees, had arrived well before she came. There were professors and dignitaries from hundreds of miles around. The woman was to teach a handful of student performers chosen by the faculty. The class began quietly. The woman artist tried to put the young musicians at ease. She spoke of willingly submitting one's skill and mastery to bringing forth the pathos and meaning from the heart of the music itself."

The old woman sighs, then continues:

"It was what happened at the close of the day that has lingered with me for so long. In the customary question period, the students and scholars became caught up in outdoing one another. Several extremely technical questions were briefly but thoroughly answered. Then, as sometimes happens on these occasions, a fever fell over the auditorium. The questions became abstract and belaboured.

"In her steady way, the woman artist began to turn away the questions. 'No,' she said to this one, 'that denies the spirit of the day.' 'No,' to another, 'I am not an expert in that area, but perhaps,' she wondered, 'might there be someone in the audience who is?' After several more questions had been turned away, the woman expressed concern that the soul of the music was being lost.

"There was a rustle of unrest. The questions abruptly ceased. The dean of the conservatory thanked the woman artist and brought the master class to a close. As the audience emptied down the aisle and out the rear door, the woman crossed over again to where the worn, brown satchel sat on the floor. She folded her sweater into it.

A sense of identity

"Several of the young women performers lingered on the stage . . . tried to engage the woman again in questions. She answered only one, with the simplest and briefest of answers . . . then started to say that she was tired. But the questioners had already left, in haste and disappointment.

"I saw there were two more young women still waiting in the shadows. One asked if she might help the woman artist with the satchel. She looked very surprised . . . hesitated for a moment. Then she quietly asked if they would like to join her for a cup of tea while she waited for her train."

The wind blows . . . leaves fall more quickly around us as the old woman speaks:

"I have wondered, all these years, at the presence that woman had, there at the close of the day. She knew so truly who she was and the value of what she gave. She did not make herself give more. I am afraid my own tendency would have been so different, young, then, as I was, and eager for success!

"All day, before an erudite audience, she had reached out with her warm generativity to inspire the younger musicians, offered her consummate artistry. Then, as the late afternoon faded into evening, she entered another realm.

"That one moment has influenced profoundly my whole life as a woman. It was as if I felt the very ground underneath me shift. I glimpsed for the very first time that other realm a woman might choose in which to live her life . . . a different mode to bring meaning to her than goal-directed accomplishment."

The old woman reaches out her hand . . . catches a leaf as it falls:

"All these years, I have wondered, what became of those young women . . . the first two, so disappointed that the woman artist refused to be other than she was. And the courage of those last two who remained . . . while all the others left!

"I have wondered if they could see, already at their age, the choices she had made: her brilliant development in the Yang realm yet her grounded return to the Yin? I hoped the intelligence and grace with which she fulfilled her task might help those young women strike their own roots in that Feminine ground."

I sit listening to the wind, in wonder at its power to freshen or devastate. In wonder, also, at the Masculine energy working in a woman that can enliven her development or completely dominate it . . . Can help her recognize her worth, or keep her from ever knowing who she truly is.

The wind blows
           . . . blows.
                       Leaves fall.

A sense of identity

How might your life have been different if, as a young woman, struggling to find out who you were, you had known of a special place that helped you ground yourself? If you had pulled your warmest sweater from the hook beside the door . . . and set off, all alone.

And, as you walked in the gathering dusk down the loneliest part of your path, you felt the chill of evening . . . and drew your sweater more closely around you . . . until, finally, as you drew nearer to that special place, you stopped and stood quietly breathing in the stillness.

And the silence and the darkness helped you be present to yourself.

How might your life be different?

A *sense of sustenance*

The wind blows . . .
        . . . chill and wild.

I put a log on the fire, glad to be warm and safe, thankful for this time of quiet to reconnect with myself . . . remembering another winter evening, long ago, when I sat quietly by the fire. My children, very young then, slept peacefully in the next room.

That evening, for the first time, I had read of an experiment that left a deep impression on me, of baby monkeys given a choice between a wire or soft mother. The wire figure had a mechanical apparatus that dispensed a feeding . . . the soft form, only a cushioned lap and pillowed body to lean against. The babies who survived best were those who chose the soft mother.

Sitting alone there, that night, I wondered if my children would know to choose the soft mother in their lives. Had they received enough nurture to know what truly would sustain them? enough elemental holding and touching to know how to care for their lives? Now, many years later, I sit in the stillness again . . . and I watch the fire, and think of our lives and the lives of women today . . . of the myriad choices open to us. And I wonder if we know how to choose what truly will sustain us.

The wind blows an icy blast . . .
        . . . drives sleet against the window.

I shiver as I consider the changes in the last few generations. Our grandmothers did not have the opportunities open to us now. If a woman wanted or needed to hold a position outside the home, she had to present herself in a Masculine image. There was little conscious understanding of the Archetypal Feminine. Women undervalued themselves and the nurturing roles they filled. Only the wire mother was known.

Four women speak of this. The first is quite young: *"I am so confused as I try to sort things out. As long as I work extended hours, have no time to reflect or feel, I can endure my life. After all, I tell myself, I've more than fulfilled Mother's aspirations.*

"She taught her three daughters her most important rules:
    1. Keep all options open.
    2. Make only goal-directed choices.
    3. Hold to universal ideals.

"But when I overhear other women speaking about their lives, I feel scared and hollow. They seem to settle into their lives in a way I've never allowed myself . . . always struggling to keep every single option open.

"I feel a longing for a woman's life I have never known, that my mother never knew, either. In my very worst moments, I grasp frantically at all the citations and awards, trying to draw comfort from somewhere, from anywhere, at all."

The second woman to speak is a little older than the first: *"Everything in my past had been only a reflection of things outside myself . . . clothing and decor, hairstyle and restaurants, even the company we kept. Everything chosen to be fashionable. Nothing reflected me!*

"I had been offered a position of power and prestige and feared that my husband wanted me to accept it. An old voice inside me said it was imperative to move ahead, and I wanted to understand where that voice actually came from. Was it really my husband's?

"I went to my mother and sister, wanting to be listened to by women's ears. But they wouldn't hear my pain. Mother, especially, was adamant, 'If you don't take this job, you'll hold your husband back!'

"I emerged from that encounter wounded, but alive, feeling a terrible failure. Then an image from an old dream suddenly came to me of a woodland spring flowing with life, but covered with a rusty wire grate. No one could reach its waters. Just like our family's way: the life flowing underneath blocked by a calendar pencilled full of events that offered no real sustenance.

"As I sat and closed my eyes, I realized how barren the lives of my mother and sister were. I felt a wave of compassion for our whole Feminine process. My mother, unable to acknowledge my pain because her own had never been acknowledged. My sister and I, never helped to embrace ourselves or our ordinary lives.

"Oh, if only my husband knew how I questioned the whole idea of this more important job . . . of being away so much, leaving the care of our home to strangers . . . abandoning the intimacy of the life I had finally found.

"I tried to think of a way to tell him how much my mornings meant to me
    . . . the special quality of quietness
        in the empty, dark kitchen
            . . . soft flutter of wings at the feeder
                . . . the rustle of pages in my journal.
    . . . Suddenly I knew how to say it so he would be able to hear me."

A sense of sustenance

The third woman, still older, listens, then begins to speak:

"I think I always chose the wire mother in my life. Even my dreams showed me employed at the Department of Labor, working unrelentingly for ambition and glory rather than to sustain the basic stuff of life. I could never play or rest, and I distrusted any woman who did.

"How strange, when I have always felt so impatient and awkward with women, that there is suddenly a mysterious old woman in my dreams, who welcomes me into a circle of women! Is it possible that she can help me change that unrelenting side of myself? . . . help me find a way of belonging among women, of belonging in my life?"

The oldest woman slowly nods as she reflects on her experience:

"Though all of us held demanding positions, we gathered every month. Time after time we resisted as the woman who led our group implored us to turn aside from our restless search, with its lofty spiritual quotations, and to look within ourselves. Finally at the end of a day, she asked us movingly, to simply share the experiences of our ordinary lives.

"When we gathered again the next month, two of the women had been ill. It was the time of the winter solstice . . . the darkest days of the year.

"As we entered the space the woman had prepared for us, our customary silence deepened. The light from the windows was already dim . . . the darkness worked its way. In the half-light from the candles and the fire on the hearth, we left our intellectual mode . . . finally found, within ourselves, a quieter, darker place we had not known was there.

"One woman after another, we shared our struggle against emptiness, our need to keep busy to avoid despair . . . our longing for a way of life that could more deeply sustain us.

"As the grey light at the windows grew fainter,
the room became hushed and still . . .
the candles burned low,
one woman sang a lullaby . . .
the wind hummed low in the chimney."

A sense of sustenance

How might your life have been different if there had been a place for you to go when your life was difficult and you felt utterly alone . . . a place of safety and comfort?

If a woman whom you trusted had been there to receive you . . . had listened silently, as you spoke your discouragement? And then she had covered you warmly as you curled up for a rest.

And, if she had gone out and returned with an armload of wood . . . then quietly built up the fire and sat down nearby to tend it . . .

How might your life be different?

A sense of voice

> *Late winter . . .*
>   *. . . the wind blows.*

An image from a woman's dream drifts through the cold to me:

> *"A woman stands alone, watches . . . silent . . . as the snow drifts down onto the field before her. New life stirs within her. She brings forth an egg, that vulnerable, precious symbol of her subjective truth as woman. For a moment she holds it close to her, only to have it torn away by a muscular young man. Identifying it as a football, and as his, at that, he darts down the field with it, dashes it heedlessly against a goal post. He scores his points, but annihilates the living contents of the woman's egg."*

How quickly a woman's truth can be torn away from her! She may be completely unaware of how competitively she wages a discussion, how heedlessly she scores points to dominate a conversation. And whenever a new understanding of life stirs within her, rather than being silently held and pondered in her heart, it is stolen and broadcast to the throng!

A woman speaks earnestly of this:

"I was grateful to hear the recording of the meeting with the new faculty. To hear, in my own voice, all that I have disliked in authorities from my past . . . everything in bold brush strokes, rather than with the nuance and subtlety that I know I am capable of. It was

not my Feminine ego leading the meeting at all, but my animus in a skirt.

"The faces around the table came back to me. I could see the pain in both the men and the women caused by that masculinized caricature of myself. There was the usual recrimination from my inner judges, until I remembered how little voice I had had in the past. I forgave my bravado mode. Perhaps it had seemed better than having no voice at all.

"I needed my Masculine side to help me develop myself, not just to criticize me from within. I asked for a new voice of constancy and prevailing, the modes I wished to affirm in the teachers under my direction. I wanted to speak firmly as a woman of strength with my ego grounded in the Feminine.

"Slowly I worked with my convictions, solidifying here, softening there. Suddenly I was filled with the feelings I had pushed away . . . with how much I cared for the work . . . for the children that we teachers all loved!

"The morning of the next meeting I laid the agenda aside and prayed that I could speak from my heart."

A second woman speaks:

"Old friends could not understand the difficulty I had coming into my own. All of the family women were expected to be like Great-grandmother. Only our brightness was acknowledged! She was still stylish and slender at ninety and a brilliant conversationalist. She corrected us all on grammar and accuracy of detail.

"Although I had grown professionally, I was disappointed in my presentations. My crisp, amusing style rarely touched the women in the audience.

"One evening, as I spoke, an image came to me of a spectator at a tennis match who focused on me for only an instant, then on the opposite court, as I started a sentence from within myself, then listened helplessly while my other voice ended it in an opposite mode. I could speak for only a moment before my animus stole the spotlight, engaging with the women in the audience so convincingly that I ended up addressing only their Masculine side.

"When I dreamed, that night, of Great-grandmother, victorious in a tennis outfit, I knew I must find a mentor from the Feminine realm!

"She was many years older than I, and very different from our family women. It took me a long time to speak with her, because I felt so confused and ashamed. She asked me to respect my confusion and allow myself to be in my muddle until some clarity emerged. She said it might be important not to impose anything more from the outside. 'Perhaps your great-grandmother's style was perfect to express her own life . . . but is not capable of expressing yours.'

"Her words gave a permission I had never been granted before. In the next presentation I let myself speak from my muddle. It was not swift and clever, as before. But perhaps it was not as slow and ponderous as I had feared it would be. What was important to me was that, for the very first time, I knew I was deeply received by the women listening to me."

A third woman sits in reflection before she begins to speak:

"My own experience has been so different, perhaps because I am older. I had begun to write of our individuation process as women. Acquaintances asked how the work was progressing and asked if they might see it.

"After only a few pages were read, the protests quickly began: Very nice work, indeed, but it must be reframed. The line is too fine, too lunar. It must be bolder, more declarative. It needs a completely different voice!

"Footsteps retreated down the driveway . . . car doors slammed shut.

"That weekend I lay in bed with flu, feverish and lost. The outer situation mirrored the chaos within . . . a female cardinal flew against the window, hour after hour, with a dull thud.

"My heart hurt under my ribs, and if I had not known so well how my body has always expressed my emotional pain, I would have feared that I was suffering a heart attack. With the fever, scenes of failure from my whole life passed before my eyes. 'Weighed in the balances and found wanting,' thundered my old inner judges . . . 'the wrong mode . . . the wrong way . . . wrong.' As wrong-headed as that lady cardinal hurtling herself against the window.

"As I neared the very bottom of the chaos, I heard only the last sentence from several days before: 'It needs a different voice . . . a completely different voice.'

"My heart grew quieter. With the grey dawn came a solitary whisper . . . 'But this is my voice!' I had laboured so long to develop its steadfast measure and balance, worked so diligently to quietly bring it forth. This was the only voice I had. There was no other.

"I slept.

"In the days that followed, I chastised myself many times. Why was I not more forthright, bolder, as the acquaintances asked? Why was I . . . only as I was? And then a memory came of a painful, patriarchal attitude: An attitude that invalidates a woman whenever

she seeks to express her subtle awareness as woman . . . leaves her struggling to bring forth her subjective experience in a hull of objectivity, an empty shell of words.

" 'No wonder,' I thought, 'that a woman sometimes adopts a Masculine voice as she speaks. No wonder she loses touch with her most poignant feeling values. And, worst of all, no wonder that a woman so often speaks her truth in a voice that is not her own . . . leaves her deepest Feminine wisdom mute, unvoiced, unheard.'

"The flu lingered several days. At last I felt well enough to be back in the woods one afternoon towards dusk. The light was soft . . . the late-winder woods, subtle hues of browns and greys.

"I sat for a long time watching the branches silhouetted against the darkening sky. Slowly, a tired awareness emerged within me . . . that all I wanted to do in my lifetime was to try . . . try to speak my truth as woman . . . to say it in my own voice."

I sit listening to the wind.
. . . the wind listens back to me.

A sense of voice

How might your life have been different if, as a young woman struggling to find your voice . . . in despair that you might never be able to say what you knew inside . . . there had been a place for you to begin to speak as a woman?

If you had been received into a circle of women, and during the silence, the women had let you speak . . . had let you speak over and over, as your words slowly came together . . . if they had listened deeply and attentively to your emerging voice?

And, how might it have been different for you, if you had seen, that day, in the faces of the women sitting there in the circle . . . in the still older faces of the women standing slightly behind them in the shadows . . . the pride and respect they felt as they heard your young woman's voice?

How might your life be different?

A *sense of sacredness*

The wind softens . . .
          . . . winter thaws.

In earliest springtime of each year, a group of women gathered in a small mountain town where there was a healing spring. It had become their custom to repair to the baths for purification and cleansing. They offered up any malady or woundedness to the powerful mineral waters.

For several years, whenever the group gathered, a ritual had taken place. As the women first assembled, a candle was lighted and a small statue placed in its light. It was a figure of a woman, wrought in brass and bronze, her hair a twisted braid of burnished copper down her back.

The statue had been found at the bottom of a chest brought back from India by the missionary great-uncle of one of the women. In the circle cast by the candle, the presence of the statue drew the women back in time . . . to a time, long ago, when the earth was still held sacred . . . to a way of being with the earth and their own Feminine nature that the women had not lived out, but dimly sensed within themselves, waiting to be reborn.

The women gathered throughout the year in several different places. There was a concern that the statue would be damaged in travel. A small, silken bag was sewn to protect it, and another, of a sturdier fabric, as covering for the first. Eventually, a third was added. The statue was well protected.

At the opening of each retreat, the yarn holding the bags closed was slowly untied and the statue carefully placed at the center of the circle. Every springtime, the woman who led the group gave each woman a gift to help keep the power of the ritual alive within her throughout the coming year.

The small cloth bags given that springtime as remembrances of the ritual were replicas of the bags holding the statue. The gifts were placed on the pillows at night while the women slept. The first woman to awaken and open her gift came in quietly to say her thanks for her "first and only Goddess bag." She wondered aloud how she would fill it. The name seemed fitting, and the gifts were remembered as the Goddess bags.

Later that same morning, the women sat on a terrace looking out over the woods. They spoke of the meaning, for each of them, of receiving the empty bag. What would each woman place into it from her own uniqueness and life?

A woman prepared to speak, brushed a strand of dark hair from her face:

"I offer into this silken bag the whole of my life as woman . . . joy and suffering both . . . all that is sacred to me: the smooth, flat stone from the day on the beach when my husband last told me he loved me, a few days before he died . . . The old damask napkin from the day I took tea with my great-grandmother, when she was ninety-two . . . Two dried flowers, the red, from the day my first daughter was born, and the lavender, from the day I thought I would die from the pain of her death."

The woman bowed her head. The woman sat in silence around her, as witness to her pain.

The youngest woman spoke, her chestnut hair aglow in the soft spring light:

"Suddenly, I see the depth of the woundedness in my woman-hood. I would not have thought, before, of honouring our sorrows or valuing our wounds . . . of holding anything of the Feminine sacred. I realize that those of us so wounded will suffer the gravest doubts in placing anything of ourselves into the silken bag.

"I offer into it the wounding in my Masculine side. My fears, when I was young, that I could not achieve in the world. And, later, an opposite wound, as my life was devoured by work. Into this silken bag, I offer the one-sided judgement that keeps me, even now, from respecting my own suffering, that fills me, instead, with shame for ever having suffered . . . shame, failure, and condemnation for having done my whole life wrong."

A slender woman listened thoughtfully, hand on her grey-blonde hair:

"I pray that we offer up our habitual denigration of our own Feminine nature . . . the denigration of ourselves that leaves us unable or unwilling to endure suffering, even the suffering necessary to discover our own souls.

"I offer up the impatience that makes us try to rip forth full-blown the answers to our lives, rather than trusting them to bring themselves forth from the Self in their own time. I offer this up and pray that a sense of quiet forbearance may be returned to us all."

The sun was low in the sky. The wind blew softly through the nearby trees.

A sense of sacredness

The oldest woman began to speak, fell silent . . . sighed:

"I didn't expect to live so long, to see such change before I died. Into this silken bag I offer a wounding of great poignancy that I see in woman after woman: a pushing and pressing at ourselves, a coldness towards our own pain . . . an expectation of ourselves to be invulnerable.

"I feel a deep concern for the lack of human kindness that I see among us . . . for an attitude that meets suffering from a safe, crisp platform of solutions rather than witnessing its truth from within our own experience of pain."

The slanting rays of the setting sun shone on her silver hair.

"Into this silken bag, I offer all that has been most scorned of the Archetypal Feminine realm . . . that it may be redeemed and healed and become most sacred to us all."

I listen in wonder
. . . spring returns.

How might your life have been different if, ever since you were a young girl, you remembered sitting alone one day when an old woman suddenly appeared? If she had spoken in a strange sing-song voice . . . of listening to the wind and thinking of the lives of woman . . . "of the past, how far our grandmothers came, of the future, open before us." And if, as the old woman spoke . . . she took out a piece of soft old cloth that you knew was silk . . . and she began to sew.

If the old woman had said she was making a little bag for you . . . and that you must offer into it all that would reflect your own image to yourself as daughter to the Great Mother. And then she had said words that you did not quite understand, "Fill it from your conscious woundedness, from your deepest awareness as woman, and lastly, from your joy."

Then, if she had looked deeply into your eyes, and said very quietly that, as you made your offerings into the silken bag, the bag of the Goddess, also, was being filled anew. "It is our sacred task to offer into this bag . . . all that will bring a new sense of the Feminine to heal and sustain us all."

How might your life have been different?

I sit listening

as the wind

asks its eternal questions:

What will our generation of women

pass on to our daughters?

What will be our legacy

to the daughters

of our great-granddaughters?

And the earth

murmurs her response:

Answer yourself . . .

. . . yourself.

Her Work
With The
Masculine
Within Her

Welcoming her energy

A May breeze murmurs from the meadow
. . . wafts of lilies-of-the-valley
. . . memories of spring commencements.

An image drifts to me:

A group of women of many ages gathers in the bright spring sunlight, young women in caps and gowns, their mothers and their teachers. A slender, blonde woman stands up, adjusts her doctoral robes . . . briefly touches the hands of the women next to her . . . looks at the young women seated around them:

"We mothers and teachers have asked you here, hoping to share our experience of our animus energy with you younger women. We are so proud of you! You have marshalled this wonderful energy so well to complete your studies, prepare for your professions!"

She nods to the black woman sitting nearest her, also in doctoral robes: *"We were remembering how it felt as our own Masculine energy first appeared: our lofty spiritual longings . . . our beautiful adolescent hero-worship of brilliant and beloved teachers . . . our sense of justice emerging . . . and our fearsome goal-directedness!"*

❖ ❖ ❖

As a young girl begins to grow up, the animus awakens within her. It brings bursting energies, a sense of power and purpose not present to her before. Now she must discipline this energy as she seeks to distinguish herself in academics, athletics, artistry: in all areas of achievement and accomplishment.

At this time, the daughter temporarily needs to separate from the mother to develop her animus powers. She must cut her roots from the Feminine ground and make a fearful crossing to the Masculine. During this crossing, the animus draws the girl as far away from the Feminine as she will ever be.

Now the girl needs a Masculine role model in the outer world for her newly-awakening animus. The encouragement from her father or male teachers is essential, especially if her mother has not worked with her own Masculine energy. The absence of this encouragement results in exaggerated feelings about the Masculine and an abstractedness that does not allow the girl to ground herself: a vacuum rather than a solidness in her feelings for herself as a woman.

❖ ❖ ❖

"When women professionals of our age were growing up," the blonde woman continues, *"we identified with our fathers or male teachers. I didn't want anything to do with the diffuse Feminine ways of my mother or her friends."*

The black woman by her side interrupts laughingly: *"I'm sure that I was headstrongly anti-feminine as I identified with my Masculine side. I was enjoying its power, and I was strutting its stuff!"*

Then she smiles across the group at her own daughter in cap and gown: *"How lucky you young women are to have the understanding of mothers who went through these stages of development themselves.*

"If the mother can remember that her daughter's struggle is against the entire Feminine realm, and not against her personally, she may be able to provide a container for the struggle that is broad enough that her daughter will not need to make a complete schism between them.

"By lending loving support, the mother may be allowed to serve as mentor for this new energy . . . may provide compass, charts, and sea anchor for her daughter's maiden voyage through these troubled and murky waters . . . May be allowed, to guide what may finally emerge as radiant qualities of leadership and excellence in her daughter's adult womanhood.

"But if the mother is unclear in her own relationship with her animus, unable to develop her talents or to find her voice, the situation will be painful for all. The Masculine energy will act out in chaotic disruption of the relationship, as mother and daughter are locked in a power struggle, turning household peace into a shambles. Mother will be unable to understand or tolerate the undirected energy in her daughter . . . will dig in her heels on the old issues of a clean room and a modest demeanour. And the girl will be scathing in her criticism of the mother."

Another woman interrupts, visibly upset: *"If only there had been someone to help my mother and me! We were terrible to each other. I needed her love, and I think she needed mine. How I wish there had been someone to give us some understanding of what was going on!"*

The black woman nods sympathetically: *"I'm so sorry for the pain that you both suffered! If only there had been someone to help your mother see that it was temporarily your task to overthrow all of her values. The mother may be the only one with steadiness enough to help the girl gain some clarity with her obstreperous young animus.*

"If the father tries to deal with this unruly side of the daughter, he may lock into combat with it, competing and needing to conquer it, and trying to break the girl's spirit. But the mother may realize that the more spirited the girl is at this age, the more glowing her leadership abilities may be when she is fully mature.

"A mother must know, in her heart, that she represents the very ground of womanhood to which her daughter will later return, this time no longer grafted onto and sustained by the roots of the mother, but striking root, herself, in the ancient Feminine ground."

The woman pauses in thought . . . then slowly reaches out to touch the lilac by her side: *"I marvel when I remember how wonderfully my mother handled this stage of my growing up. She fostered the relationship between my father and me, made the natural attraction between us feel safe, and helped him provide a good role model for the Masculine side of me. She encouraged Father to listen to me, to help me draw my thoughts together, sometimes even to help me take a stance!*

"My mother must have known how a girl's whole sense of herself can be affected by criticism, especially if it is stinging or harsh, how the animus will pick it up and undermine her with it for years to come. For she listened so caringly to my pain."

Two women stand to respond. The first speaks:

"My father and brothers saw me as competition . . . a poor second to father, fair game to all those brothers. And my mother saw me as a threat . . . and put me out of her kitchen and study. I had no one to support me . . . no encouragement from any direction.

"I became as tough as my brothers . . . merciless to myself. My inner voice is still as nasty to me as they were. To this day, I can feel that pain and rebelliousness, as if I can't do anything anyhow, so why try? I am learning, only now, to marshall my energies and abilities in a way that gives meaning to my life. And I'm scared for the time my three little girls will need me to befriend, in them, what was never befriended in me."

The second woman speaks:

"I am so very grateful. Something quite different happened to me. A professor acknowledged me in class as I sat amidst my peers. I had presented a short paper on Aeschylus. When I finished reading, the professor looked straight at me and said, 'Miss_____ , you have a keen and subtle mind.' He was a wonderful model for the Masculine side of myself. That happened nearly forty years ago and still helps me feel secure about my skills."

A white-haired woman walks slowly into the group. She had lingered at a Grandmothers' Tea held earlier, across the meadow:

"We oldest women are so moved at what lies before you younger ones. In our time, it was taken for granted that much of a woman's development would be lived out through a man. There were stories told humorously of "my son, the doctor" when sons or husbands fulfilled what the woman was not allowed to do.

"But now, you are developing your own talents and bringing all of your gifts to flower. We oldest women want you to know that we believe in you . . . that you have the opportunities and responsibilities that can change the world!

"We send our encouragement for success in that outer realm. And we send our warmest blessing that your young woman's spirits will be nourished by striking deep roots in the inner realm of the Feminine.

"For somehow . . . somehow . . . "

. . . the breeze wafts an almost unfathomable fragrance of lily-of-the-valley as the old woman takes the hand of the slender black woman in doctoral robes, drawing the gathering into a circle:

" *. . . somehow,*" she continued, *"we old ones want you to know of a vision we have seen only dimly. Of a nobility and power and wisdom that lies within all women, but sometimes is not lived out.*

"You all know that your mothers will always be here in a circle around you as you work with your gifts. And we oldest women promise that we will be here, also, in an outer circle, holding in our hearts that ancient vision of women . . . praying that it will come alive . . . watering the roots of all of us in the Feminine ground."

The woman who had begun the morning stood up, tears sparkling in her eyes:

"And when the time comes for each of you to lovingly help your own daughter welcome her new energy, let her know that we feel her excitement, that we respect her struggle . . . that we have struggled, too.

"And that there is a place for her here with us, rooted in the ground of the Feminine!"

How might your life have been different if, once when you were a young girl . . . worried about your studies and still wanting to be helpful at home . . . your mother had quietly looked at you, one evening, and said, "It's all right, dear, I'll clear the table tonight. I know that you have a test tomorrow. Go, do what you need to prepare . . . and take a little time for yourself."

And then, if she had said, very softly, with a smile,
        " . . . later, let's look at the moon together
                . . . there's a lovely spring breeze blowing."

How might your life be different?

Embracing her encounter

I sit listening to the wind
. . . wondering and worrying
about our work with the animus.

Sometimes the Masculine side of us seems just like the men in a woman's life: she cannot get along with them and she cannot get along without them. Until she becomes aware of the Masculine energy within and consciously engages with it, it remains an autonomous force, out of her control. It keeps a woman focused on what happens around her, rather than on developing herself as deeply as she can.

The complete absence of animus energy would leave a deathly stillness . . . the woman would have no power to become who she truly could be!

There is a strong connection between a woman's animus and the men around her, like two mirrors facing each other, one inside and one outside the woman. When a woman first works to develop herself, both mirrors may seem unsympathetic. But as she grows, she will see her growth reflected in both inner and outer mirrors. As the Masculine within begins to help her express herself, the men around her begin to listen. And as she dares to speak out to the men in her daily life, the Masculine figures in her dreams reflect their growing respect.

Years ago, a group of women met to discuss this energy. We knew it was affecting our relationships with the men in our lives, and we wanted to know how to work with it. But we had no idea how to begin. And we were tired of worrying!

One woman told her own story of encountering this energy. But soon the discussion became generalized and full of puffy abstractions. By the end of the afternoon, we disbanded in disarray, taken over by the very side of ourselves we had been trying to discuss . . . As if it did not want to be exposed and have its power threatened!

How were we ever going to engage with this energy, and not just be blown about by it?

We decided to try again and stay with only our subjective sharing. A hearty woman began:

"I was raised quite traditionally. We knew nothing of women developing themselves. We identified completely with patriarchal views, expressed all the accepted attitudes. On good days, everything seemed rosy for us: nice little women staying in our places. And frighteningly unaware of our own existence as women!

"But on bad days, and in a black mood, I stood at the kitchen sink, dish cloth idly in hand, or stared listlessly over the copy machine out of my office window. The animus burst into my dreams as an intruder breaking in at the door. And it burst just as impulsively into my daily life . . . tearing at the garden, pounding at my typewriter, or scolding at my husband. And it was I who was doing it!

"I saw the same harsh qualities in every man I met, without realizing that those were the qualities of my untamed animus. It was blowing undirected and devastating all in its path. And as I tried to confront it, it called out heavy artillery. I was assailed by criticism from within and without. On the outside, from men who were actually judgemental as well as from those who were kinder. And on the inside, stinging rejection from all my old inner judges. It was a terrible time!"

She covered her face with her hands. The woman nearest her silently rested her hand on the woman's shoulder. A yellowed newspaper clipping fell from her journal onto the floor. She picked it up as she spoke:

"I cut this out many years ago and labeled it "The Energy of the Animus United Against the Woman as She Begins Her Encounter Within." It is a frightening picture. Nine or ten men in a close cadre, standing on the steps of the Supreme Court . . . their faces full of accusation and twisted into snarls. The picture reflected exactly the Masculine energy within me as it projected out and was reflected back by the men around me. So full of insults and judgement, as I began my inner work!"

A very young woman broke in:

"I'm finally figuring it out! If the men around us do not treat us with respect, then the men in our dreams treat us disrespectfully, too, and we feel badly about ourselves. Last week, I took a big risk and asked the man at the desk next to mine to pick up his share of the work. That night I dreamed of a man helping me carry a burden. But this surely was not how to begin!"

An older woman laughed and reached out to touch the younger woman's hand: *"We begin however we can! None of us really knows how. I began to encounter the animus at a time when I was very critical of myself and others. I knew something was at me and I had to communicate with it.*

"So, in an image, I summoned all of the male figures from my dreams. Then I wondered if I could be less imperious. If I could not only encounter those figures but also embrace the encounter with warmth! So I invited them to a council as ambassadors and couriers. Even set out colourful banners and flags to mark their seats.

Embracing her encounter

"One by one, I encountered each of those threatening figures who had judged me so harshly in my dreams. With dignity and formality, I told them that they must change. It was my life as a woman that was to be lived and their cooperation was needed. Then I asked the more encouraging figures, helpful teachers and mentors from the past, to take the others in hand. I asked them to be like knights preparing the young squires, teaching them how to serve with devotion and honour, and charging them with a trust to be my protectors and aides. Then I embraced each one of them and offered my heartfelt thanks."

The women sat quietly for a few moments.

Gradually, we realized how different this had been from our discussion the day before. We felt a keen appreciation for the women who had spoken. Because of their efforts to embrace their own encounter within, each of us was starting to understand how to begin the encounter within ourselves. We sat in silence together for a very long time. And we knew that their stories would stay with us.

❖ ❖ ❖

Slowly over the years, a woman's awareness of herself deepens as, again and again, she encounters the Masculine within. Now she can ask it to cease its judgement. She can call upon its strengths.

Finally it is available to help her develop herself!

How might it have been different for you, when you were at odds with your closest friends . . . confused and in conflict within, if there had been a place for you, where you could be received by a woman whom you respected? And she had listened as you told her how cut off you felt from yourself.

If the woman had quietly laid a fire and slowly begun to teach you a strange, new kind of dialogue . . . speaking your thoughts and feelings to the cut-off part of yourself that did not seem to understand . . . then to sit in silence, listening for a response? And you had been surprised at how that mysterious other part of you listened . . . and amazed to hear its answer!

And, as the fire burned low, you sat hugging your journal . . . knowing you had just begun an encounter that would continue all of your life . . .

How might your life be different?

Bringing forth her feeling values

The wind blows so insistently
I cannot hear the earth
erupting underneath.
Cut off, I listen
. . . listen.

When a woman uses her energy only to reinforce what is outside of herself, she becomes cut off from her depths. Her own feelings and life values become inaccessible to her. She molds herself to external standards and loses touch with her individuality. She is cut off from all that is uniquely hers that could nourish her and those around her . . . cut off from the creative, new answers within her so badly needed in the world today. Cut off from her deeper sense of life, from the wisdom of her own unconscious, she lives in an arid, approvable way.

And her depths become enraged!

The whole wellspring of womanly creativity within her is furious for not being tapped. And the greater the individuality and insight that have been dammed up, the greater the rage. For what is within must flow out: her feelings and life values, all that the woman cares about and knows, most deeply, to be true.

❖ ❖ ❖

Five women sat in a rough cabin sheltered from the turbulent wind. They spoke of the difficulty women sometimes have in expressing themselves. The first woman had just returned from a journey:

"I was aware of the anguish of women in areas where I trav-
elled . . . women unable to express their feelings or bring forth their
Feminine values. I thought of an old text, hidden away for centuries
before it re-emerged:

> 'If thee brings forth what is within,
>   what thee brings forth will heal thee.
> If thee does not bring forth what is within,
>   what is forbidden to come forth will destroy thee.'

"I remembered a more ancient bringing forth as woman, during the menses, closest then to her own nature, knelt on the earth to offer
it the gift of her own blood. She offered herself to the cycles of nature . . . knowing that nature would respond and pour forth its blessing in return.

"I wondered if we women might offer our blood again, in a
symbolic way . . . trusting that life itself will pour forth its blessings in
response. If we might offer our blood to replenish our society with the
Feminine values that are so cut off . . . values of devotion to the earth
and to the individual . . . the values of the deeper Self."

An older woman paused in thought before she began to
speak:

"I escaped and am settled now, in my second life! It has been a
long journey. My origins were very traditional, yet I had managed to
get an education, in spite of the attitudes against it.

"One night, in a dream, a woman came to me, so full of frus-
tration and fatigue that she could only lean her forehead against the
frame of a door. She held it there, mute and tearless . . . unable to enter
or leave.

Bringing forth her feeling values

"I awoke and recognized her as the suffering Feminine in my-self. I had found a job within the given structure and called it my 'Cleft in the Rock.' It seemed to offer survival, though little personal space.

"But later, there was a second dream of a woman's body crushed amidst rocks . . . and I knew that those were the rocks of that bloodless, impersonal system that could never make room for me . . . Never make room for anything from the Feminine realm!"

A third woman, a painter and musician, recalled her own ancestry:

"Those black-garbed forebears of mine had required strict conformity of behaviour and belief. I grew up playing every phrase to someone else's cadence. So taught to disregard feelings that I never knew what I felt!

"One day as I painted, all the passion of my blocked womanhood broke through. It poured forth onto the canvas in blazing reds and oranges. My whole body joined in a primitive dance.

"With arms flung wide, I danced until every cell of my being knew that I was alive . . . alive to the joy and intensity within me . . . alive to myself, to life!"

Suddenly the women rushed to the window. An old wall lay toppled before the changing wind.

❖ ❖ ❖

When they returned to their seats, the fourth woman spoke:

"My grandmother, my mother, and me . . . only allowed to smile and agree. Only able to affirm what was initiated around us, never able to initiate ourselves.

"If my grandmother ever disagreed, she got upset and hysterical. And my mother swang between hysteria and an opinionated animus, with no grounded Feminine ego between them . . . Enraged that the men could never hear what she was unable to say.

"Caught between those modes, I was depressed and cut off from myself, with no energy for the causes I had served only half a year before! And my judging animus did its foul double-play, first damning me for my depression, then berating me for having served so long what had not served me.

"All those generations of women in my lineage using our energies in service to a system that had so little awareness of Feminine feelings and values." The woman spoke with a quiet intensity, gripping the arms of her chair: *"A woman counsellor came. She asked me to trust my feelings, even my depression, as my deepest truth.*

"She asked me to respect my rage, not identify with it. But to honour it as holding within itself all of the ancient Feminine, so long dormant, neglected . . . forbidden, for so long, to come forth.

Bringing forth her feeling values

"She asked me to stay with my pain, not let my animus invalidate it . . .

Helped me shriek it in wordless, guttural cries
. . . paeans of despair to the gods:

The anguish of suppressed feeling values
of my mother and her mother before her,

of lost devotion to matter,
lost Feminine sovereignty,

of rain-forests felled,
waters spilt with oil,
. . . the anguish of the earth herself!

"She asked me to imagine the significance if woman could heal the split between her inner Masculine development and her unlistened-to womanly values. The significance if each woman would be willing to consciously suffer her own share of the anguish that tells us something is vastly wrong in the values of this world today.

"To imagine the significance, if each woman were willing to bear the pain and isolation that must be endured, each time, to bring our values to expression. The significance, if each of us would pour out our devotion, as our ancient sisters poured out their blood. Pour out our passion and devotion, and await the response . . . as the ancient Feminine Archetype brings forth her values anew!"

The fifth woman tells her dream:

"Near the edge of the woods a group of people gathers. They stand hushed and reverent.

Suddenly there is a tremor, a pulsating beneath the surface. From cracks and crevices, blood erupts from the earth . . . rises aloft to the heavens . . . returns to the earth as rain.

The group throngs into the clearing. With heads upturned and arms outstretched, they raise a joyous cry: 'The blood has returned to the land!' "

How might your life be different, if you had a place to go, whenever you were overwhelmed by the power of your feelings? If you could be received by women gathered in a circle . . . and helped to witness your feelings . . . and to trust their truth?

If the women would build up the fire and let you dance out your feelings . . . your pain and anguish and hurt . . . even your wordless rage.

And, as the fire burned low and you rested from your dance, you could look into the glowing embers . . . and wonder how it might have been different for your mother and grandmother before you, if they, also, had been received by women, long before you were born. If women, then, could have helped them trust that their feelings served a purpose . . . helped them know that their feelings might bring truth to bear where it was needed?

How might the lives of every one of us be different?

Honouring her intuition

*The wind blows clouds across
the strange, dark face of the moon
. . . hardly there at all
against the last, piercing rays of the sun.*

The element of the Feminine most difficult to comprehend is the lunar spirituality of the Feminine intuition . . . the strange, ineffable beauty of the dark face of the moon.

A woman's drawing showed this: one delicate, dark line on an otherwise empty page . . . a woman's face in profile, one tear falling on her cheek. The woman named it *The Nothing Against the Something,* this ephemeral lunar quality of woman's intuition . . . elusive, mute and weeping . . . impossible to articulate.

Impossible . . . for the intuition offers itself in images, not words. What the intuition grasps cannot be held in the hand. Moreover, modern society places little value on "things unseen." And the more distinctly Feminine a woman's intuition, the more it lingers in shadow beside the brightness of her inner Masculine. The subtler her gift, the greater her struggle to bring it forth. The animus will make it seem hardly there at all!

If older women around her have not learned to trust their own intuition, they will be unable to help the younger woman bring forth her gift. The intuition, by nature, is easily dismissed. The woman's Masculine side will undermine any intuitive awareness she has, pointing out the achievements of others in more identifiable realms. She will feel that her intuitive gifts are nebulous and insubstantial, tell herself she should have been at least a tax attorney, if not a superb cook.

The intuitive woman is caught between two aspects of the animus. On the one side, the Judging Patriarch invalidates her subjective perceptions. He holds up before her the already established spiritual belief systems that make no room for the woman's uniquely personal intuitive gift.

The woman's inner Patriarch projects out onto others and seems to come at the woman as disregard from those around her, demanding that she remain silent. She will continually ally herself with groups that do not recognize her. The more vibrantly the woman's own vision presses to emerge, the more vehemently the Patriarch will thunder: "Condemned if you dare to speak your truth!"

Across from the Judging Patriarch stands an immature Peter Pan who forever refuses to grow up. He will not let the woman take herself seriously or help her develop her gifts to challenge the established order. And the more directly the woman's intuition speaks from the true Feminine, the more the Peter Pan within will engage in a frenzy of activity to distract her from bringing it forth.

The inner Peter Pan makes the woman see her own abilities in others rather than in herself. Dapper and debonair, he runs her all over town to lectures and workshops, seeking outside herself the depths she cannot own within . . . keeps her an admiring disciple of the vision she sees in others. Finally, he drops her at her doorstep, empty and exhausted!

Caught between these two aspects of the animus, the woman is in terrible pain. For the intuition is a woman's strongest inherently Feminine component: when she cannot own these depths, she is left hollow, robbed of her essence. The truest voice within her seems condemned by those around her and is so unclear inside her that she cannot bring it forth.

If only the woman could realize how deeply her gift is needed! For her intuition is the living connection, the conduit to the Self. Through this conduit flows the essence of life that keeps the soul of humanity alive!

When a society is not nourished by a connection to the deeper Self, it can easily be taken over. Oppressive mass belief systems appear that lead to barrenness and spiritual sterility. At this point, the intuitive woman must realize her true responsibility as visionary to the society around her: for only the freshness and life of her intuition can bring forth the new message needed to refute the stagnation and barrenness of the established order.

Now, the woman must have the courage to work with her vision, no matter how fragmentary it may seem. She must challenge the crushing oppression from the Judging Patriarchs within that have condemned her to silence, and demand of the immature Peter Pan that he help bring her vision to words. She must know the truth of what is there, inside, and let go of worrying whether she will ever be approved or even heard.

Now, the moment has come for the woman to own her maturity and authority. It is time for her to feel her compassion for the society around her and to take her stance. At this moment she must speak, whether her voice tremble or her whole body shake! Let her remember the ancient Feminine seers who wept as their vision poured through them, or the Quakers who trusted the shaking as a sign of truth being revealed.

Finally, the woman must reach down within, and out to those around her, and let flow what has been locked inside!

❖ ❖ ❖

A group of women gathered to hold their concerns in the light. The woman who first broke the silence was a poet and painter:

"My animus reflected so clearly the men in my family lineage . . . men of power in the world, who found women charming and curious, but of little consequence beyond that.

"My own father, who was an admiral, was never able to understand the pain it caused my mother when war called him to sea. There was no comprehension of a deeper Feminine nature . . . no tolerance for darkness or suffering in any form whatever.

"Even after I graduated from Harvard, my overly-rational animus would not honour my womanly intuition . . . would not grant recognition to my most essential part.

"Trying to fill the hollow, I studied comparative religions, the spiritual vision of others. But even then, the animus intervened in an insidious way, accused me of neglecting the family. I imagined myself as a Mother Rabbit, standing forever on the porch, waving her apron in welcome to her husband and children . . . but never able to bid adieu to have quiet time for herself.

"Two decades later, I fought cancer, just as my mother had. Her illness had left a terrible void. For in trying to fulfill family patterns that denied illness or darkness, she had fought cancer valiantly throughout my childhood, simply disappearing into the hospital without leaving a trace whenever her suffering became acute.

"And I suffered, years later, from dreadful attacks of panic that I would disappear, too, unless I could bring forth what was locked inside.

"I began to paint my anguish, the bitter struggle amidst suffering of my deepest Feminine nature so rejected by my animus.

"Finally, after many months, a sign of transformation appeared: the figure of a black Christ on the canvas, the Masculine who knew my suffering. Knew the struggle to embrace one's inner truth in the face of the establishment . . . the Nothing Against the Something so deep in the Feminine vision."

There was a long silence. Another woman spoke quietly of her father, a powerful figure whose criticism was painful because his prominence in the world made him seem always right:

"All of Mother's energy went to Father's support. There was no one to help me understand all that was inside me. The only realities recognized were the polls and the press.

"As a girl, I feared I was crazy as I saw behind the scenes or listened underneath. And as a grown woman, I was terrified that what I sensed inside would never be brought forth, but would perish . . . a strangled scream.

"Finally, years later, a quiet nurse confirmed for me the healing energy flowing in my hands. She said it was the same power held by ancient women healers as well as by nurses today.

"And finally, I have realized that, although it may seem strange to some, my hands and intuition know what they know. This has to stand as my only truth against inner or outer condemnation. For everything most alive in me and in the children I teach is flourishing!"

Honouring her intuition

How might your life have been different if, when you were a young woman, uncertain about something you could not begin to explain, there had been a place where you could be with older women? If, as you sat with those women . . . they had quietly turned towards you and begun to speak . . . as if they sensed your gifts and what was troubling you? And you knew that, somehow, they knew about uncertainty themselves.

If, one by one, the women had spoken into the silence, of women's intuition, her sensitivity to life, and of a woman's awareness of her own sensitivity . . . of her conscious willingness to open to it, and to the pain it might bring? And the women spoke of the strength that they knew was required for a woman to choose to remain vulnerable to her own sensitivity.

If, as you listened that day, you sensed the intensity and power in the women's silence . . . as if their simply sitting quietly, holding all of this in awareness, was allowing the same awarenesses to quietly unfold within you . . .

How might your life be different?

Distinguishing her life

The wind drops.
The fragrance of fresh-mown hay
drifts across the fields
. . . the first harvest of late summer.

I sit listening . . . remembering a woman whose life was rich in
harvest. Supervisor in a large state hospital, she was retiring,
after years of service, with recognition and honours. She received official citations . . . and a cat to keep her company.

Things seemed to be going smoothly. She redirected
her energy from the hospital to her private practice . . . and, of
course, tended the cat. Oh, perhaps she was working a bit
more than she wished, she said, *"but things would even out."*

And, yet, the situation seemed to shift the other way!

Years before, she had known that her father, a man of
the open plains, was terribly proud of his daughter . . . his sons
came ten years later . . . and he worked to develop the skills
and bravery of his golden-haired little girl. The story she remembered most poignantly, told with pride and pain, was of
the day she had circled the house, at her father's command, to
test her endurance and courage . . . barefoot in the snow.

As the girl grew, she went on to discipline herself in
many different directions:

"I always did well in school. Like many women of my age, I
was taught to use the mind in a purely rational way . . . as if life
could be understood logically. But I had no understanding or tolerance
for my own needs for nurture or rest. That inner driving force allowed

me as little softness as my father had. During the years of my marriage, I had my husband install light bulbs in the garden and weeded far into the night.

"I have mourned so long the difficulty I have had in relating to women. As a young girl, my feeling needs were left unsupported. Mother took pride in my mind and accomplishments, but she related very little to the rest of my development. There was a deep well of undifferentiated feeling within me, full of isolation and pain, that was never recognized by her.

"In my adolescence, I was perplexed as Mother set me the task of accomplishing her goals, while she sat chatting cozily with my more girlish girlfriends. No wonder that, years later, I was fearful of betrayal by women. As much as I longed for their closeness, I felt too alienated from the Feminine to allow myself to be received.

"With my children, also, there was difficulty. I knew they respected my abilities, for they both followed in my professional footsteps. Yet they spoke of me as an island of unrest, offering nowhere to dock, whenever they expressed concern about my personal well-being. After all, I had trained myself to manage with so little regard from others . . . the girl who ran barefoot in the snow!

"The very efficiency and capability that had always served me so well, was, of course, my undoing . . . my quiet time always stolen, since I was so able to cope. Stopped in the hospital corridors by every troubled face, on the way to every meeting . . . and always arriving late. I was at war with time, plain old Chronos time . . . I had no idea at all of what Kairos time was about.

"And then, one day, the cat ran away.

"Bereft, I knew I had to bring my life back to myself. I realized that the formality of the name I had chosen for 'Mr. Cat' reflected my reluctance to recognize my own simple creaturely needs.

"For the first time in my life, I became aware of the necessities of nurture and care . . . began to give consideration to food, took time to prepare it thoughtfully. I knew I must free myself from the compulsive false energy of an animus that knew no natural tiredness: I arranged for a series of vigorous massages . . . then for a second series, gentler than the first.

"I made a promise to myself to give time, each day, to my journal . . . dreamed of making the journey to hold my first grandchild in my arms . . . the daughter of my daughter.

"On the weekend, I walked by the river.

"I began to clear away the thousands of things I had saved, waiting for time to savour them. Beautiful dresses, now too small, that I never found occasion to wear, bought to give me a special feeling about myself as a woman. I folded them into a box and grieved for a side of myself that had never been allowed to live.

"The books were the hardest to sort. I had always thrived on reading and the world of ideas. But I knew I would never have time to uncover my own ideas of life if I were to read every one of those carefully-hoarded words.

"I sorted a lifetime of papers.

"And now I am sorting out the way I learned to use my mind, devoid of womanly knowing. The young women of my generation were taught to shunt aside feelings, the Feminine subjectivity that is our very earth and grounding. It has taken me years to recover from the *barrenness of my life . . . to finally embrace my truth, rather than to reject it.*

"*A few months ago, I heard the expression 'A Woman, Distinguishing Her Life.' I loved the two meanings it had for me: to graduate or retire with honours, distinguishing herself in that way. But also, to sort and delineate, as I have had to do, so that I could begin to see what really belonged in my life . . . distinguishing the content and meaning of my life from everything surrounding it . . . to allow the essence of my own individual life, at last, to emerge.*

"*Towards the end of the summer, late one afternoon, something happened that told me I was finding my thread. One of my women graduate students came by for a conference. We sat, for a while, towards sunset, discussing her paper and ideas, the caring we both felt for her work.*

"*Then she read me her first paragraph: 'I am exploring how the Feminine thinking function might differ from the Masculine's, how we might incorporate our new consciousness of ourselves as women with our inner Masculine side. Imagine what might happen in the next few generations if we approach our thinking with a separate womanly awareness: embrace our Feminine feeling values as the very warp of our process . . . shuttle between mind and heart to weave a wondrous, whole new fabric!'*

"*She put down her thesis and looked at me with tears, 'Thank you for your heart-mind.' "*

A fine light breeze rustles the leaves
against the darkening sky.
The tiniest star
sits twinkling on the horizon.

How might your life have been different if, late one afternoon, near the end of the summer, as you thought of the opening of school . . . of trying, again, to learn to use your mind in traditional ways . . . something wondrous had happened?

If the women who were your teachers had invited their young women students . . . even the littlest girls . . . to come to sit in a circle . . . and, of course, you sat there, too? And you sensed the excitement in the voices of those women teachers as they spoke of a different way to use your fine, young minds.

If you sat and took a deep breath and felt the wonder of it all . . . the wonder of women sitting in a circle, under the open sky, just outside the school . . . women gathered to share their wisdom with the young women in their care. And you knew, from that day forward, that nothing would be quite the same . . .

How might your life be different?

I sit listening

as the wind

asks its eternal questions:

What will our generation of women

pass on to our daughters?

What will be our legacy

to the daughters

of our great-granddaughters?

And the earth

    sings her response:

                Offer yourself . . .

                        . . . yourself.

Her Return To
Feminine Ground

Her contagion

> *I sit listening*
> *the wind blows . . .*

As a woman matures, she deepens in her knowledge of her work within . . . moves towards a closer relationship with the Self. By this time, she has worked diligently to find her inner direction, struggled to free herself from slavishly following the directives of her animus.

Yet, at this late stage, the animus exerts a counter-pull. One woman tells of her experience: *"Once again, I feel endangered by judgements from my old patriarchs, within as well as without. Now, a subtler form of judgement: after all of my work, why have I not come farther?"*

The animus, not yet won over, is making the last great effort to keep the woman focused on the outer realm, so that she cannot focus within on the realm of the deeper Self. Now, she must continuously sort herself out so that she can take her stance. For only by her efforts to choose, each time, can she release herself from bondage.

At this stage, the animus works with enormous subtlety: *"I suffer a mild contagion, as if I am running a slight fever, that keeps me apart from myself, not available to others."*

The animus puts the woman up to doing something important, without telling her what it should be . . . makes her live from outside of herself, flipping back and forth from centeredness to over-dispersed activity . . . unaware of her frenetic ambivalence or of how she betrays herself! She tries to fulfill her tasks in time that does not exist, fills out forms or addresses letters between her daily appointments. Never allows herself time enough for her freshly washed hair to dry.

The gravest danger from this contagion is the possibility that the woman will be taken over completely, as she is kept from settling into the quiet spaces she has prepared:

> *I cannot notice*
>   *the sunlight*
>   *drifting in at the window*
>   *. . . the pungence*
>   *of the scarlet chrysanthemums*
>   *on my reading table.*
> *I lose a sense of the realness and substance of my life.*
>   *Even my daily silences seem stale and contrived.*

❖ ❖ ❖

A group of women reflected on a troubling experience from the day before. One of them described it:

"A woman spoke at length . . . paragraphs of dramatic details . . . without sharing what she made of it all. At the end she asked insistently if we had understood, as if she knew how removed she had been from herself.

"As gently as we could, we told her she had been quite long. But she acted utterly destroyed, claiming hurt beyond measure, and huffily insisting that she thought this was a place for sharing! She accused us of being uncaring, then stormed away in a bluster. Although we had given our all, it was as nothing to her animus!

Her contagion

"When we gathered the next day, the woman was not with us. We realized sadly that her Masculine side might need to run its course.

"Then we tried to understand what had happened: When a woman speaks from her heart and we receive her from ours, all of us are nourished by the true feelings alive in the moment. Threatened, the Masculine side of us fears it will lose us all from its grasp and it becomes very active.

"Let me tell you an old dream:
A figure in a long grey cloak stood welcoming women into a grotto. I thought it was the cloak of an ancient priestess in a place held sacred to the Feminine. To my shock, there was a man dressed up in those robes . . . with red high heels showing beneath his hairy legs.

"That was my Masculine side! Had me go into a gathering of women acting omniscient in the very realm of the Feminine where he had no footing at all! Had me out-womaning women simply to feed his power-drive.

"That side of me can be so clever, so subtly wounding with his wit. Dismissing the women around me with little jokes and charming stories. Invalidating my Feminine feeling-values, so that I quote outer authority, while my own is entirely discounted. That side of me puts on a veneer of sentimentality. Shows a moist eye occasionally. But does not let me draw near to my real tears, which would break his hold.

"If only we knew how to gently alert a friend when we see her in the grip of that Masculine part of herself! And if only we knew how to stay so grounded in the Feminine that our own Masculine side would not be stirred into action by that side of her.

"That is the way of the animus! I sometimes think I can see a woman rise a few inches above her chair as the animus spins her up . . . and keeps all of us from being really present to her or to ourselves."

As the other women laughed, the woman brushed back her hair. *"And now I'm going to stop myself, for I know, by now, that this busy chatter often opens the door for my animus: I begin to seek attention. And then the animus flings open wide the door for all manner of behaviour.*

"Let me be silent now and find my ground again."

❖ ❖ ❖

One by one, the women entered the silence. The room grew very still. The youngest among them broke the silence. Her face, still slender and intense, shone under her greying hair:

"I never was able to make a commitment to my life. Too many fiancés, too many jobs, and even too many friends. As a creative child, I had received Mother's constant attention. Perhaps it was her own undeveloped Masculine side showering attention on me for what she had not done.

"Finally, last year, I was offered a position at a regional center for the arts, with some permanence and solidity, if I could make a commitment. Sure enough, immediately my old inner voice asked insinuatingly, 'But my dear, you'll be bored with such a provincial surrounding. What's the harm in staying free?'

Her contagion

"That evening, as I struggled with the question, an image came to me of an old nun, who had taught mime at the academy many years before. 'Hasn't that inner sorcerer stolen enough from you? What's the harm, indeed? Soon he'll steal your life!'

"My old nun looked straight at me: 'It is not enough to intellectually understand our patterns. We must engage with them and change them, or we deceive ourselves. Give up the role of being an eternally charming girl and tell your Masculine side to stop being an insubstantial boy.'

"Her grey eyes softened for a moment as they looked into mine, 'Claim your dignity and maturity and authority. Make the choice towards your deepest Self!' "

❖ ❖ ❖

The afternoon sun cast long shadows. There was silence to honour the woman's story. An older woman seated near her nodded quietly in understanding:

"Several years ago, I was invited to read my work in the town where I was born. I selected the material carefully, choosing passages that illustrated women's individuation, our movement away from outer conformity as we become ourselves.

"As the time drew near to return to my birthplace, I found myself frightened and shy . . . tempted to read, not passionately and fullheartedly as was my usual style, but like the schoolgirl those women had known fifty-five years before.

"The day before my journey, I was full of dreadful anxiety. Would I really present my own material in a sterile and 'proper' fashion? Betray this chance to witness to woman's individuation?

"When I entered the train the next day and tried to settle myself, a comforting image came . . . of a stately and beautiful actress in her role in Ibsen's Ghosts, which I had seen several seasons before. Her lines rang out, in my memory, of wishing to live a life of courage and vision, rather than to pass it in servitude to 'dead ideals and worn-out old beliefs.'

"As the waiter served coffee in the dining car, late in the afternoon, I selected the last material for my presentation. For the opening reading, I chose a poem in the voice of a mature woman:

"If I am so perpetually terrified
        of being called a bad girl,
so eternally blown about
        by the winds of my inner judges,
that I cling to any authority
        that grants me marginal approval,
then I risk that I might never, ever
        turn towards that within me
that guides and orders my existence,
        that lets the truth of my life emerge.

O! Grant me courage to become myself!"

The wind blows
        . . . leaves rustle, russet and gold.

Her contagion

How might our lives, as women, be different if there were a place for us to go when we were in dreadful conflict within and at odds with our women friends . . . when we had already struggled with our conflict and couldn't make sense out of it? A place where we could be with women more settled than ourselves . . . women who had deeply worked with the truth of their own lives.

If we could spill out to those women our confusion and feverishness . . . and they would listen quietly and gently, until we ourselves could begin to hear . . . but then they would point out clearly to us the source of our upset within?

If the honesty and patience of the women . . . and the knowing that we were heard . . . would somehow soothe our pain and allow clarity to emerge . . .

How might our lives be different?

Her possession

The wind blows mysteriously
. . . full of mesmerizing power.

As a woman works consciously with the Masculine side of herself, she learns its patterns and behaviours, begins to see, in the moment, how it influences her. Yet, even then, from time to time, she is snatched from behind . . . possessed.

The woman is the last to be aware. Her women friends or her husband are the first to feel the sting . . . and always, her poor children. All that is negative in the Feminine realm floods over the woman at this moment . . . the loathing of herself, neglect and abuse of the elemental . . . her body, family, and household! The door is open to cursing, to the nursing of old hurts, as the woman is taken over by this awesome negative power.

A woman tells her dream:

"I had been abducted and was being held captive in a room far above the earth . . . lured there by hypnotic praise.

I knew that my abductor was a terrifying destroyer of women and if I succumbed to his hypnotizing, I would become a destroyer, too!"

What can release a woman from this terrible spell? If a man tries to intervene, he may be attacked by the woman's rampaging Masculine side. For this side of a woman is only a brittle reflection of the warmth and strength of the true

Masculine and will try to destroy the outer man and dominate the situation.

Only if a man can remember not to be drawn into words, or into competition with the woman's animus, does he stand a chance of bringing her back to life.

Even her women friends face a risk from the destructive power. For when a woman is in the grips of animus possession, her true nature and feelings are inaccessible to her. She is unconscious of how hurtful her words and actions are. Only the deepest devotion from a woman friend might draw the woman back to her womanly relatedness. Through gentle nurture, the friend might be able to help the woman come back into the realm of matter, back to a wordless connection to her simple creaturely needs. By quietly attending her and expressing compassion for her pain, the friend might offer the most powerful healing of all: if the woman can weep, her tears will break the spell.

A woman spoke of the anguish brought by animus possession:

"I thought of myself as so spiritual that I was completely unconscious of my real behaviour. It was as if I were mesmerized, I rose so disdainfully above our daily life. The house was quite beneath me! I would not focus on a task. I cared so little for the material realm that I could not bring order to the matter of our lives.

"Every morning, my children went out like little disheveled ragamuffins, with everything all askew. And in the afternoon, when they returned from school, I would scream that they'd interrupted my meditation with their pedestrian concerns. While, to my evening study groups, I presented an opposite image: a self-conscious over-centeredness without any freshness or life.

"I blamed it all on my husband, who did not live up to my intellectual or spiritual ideals. He just went to work each day and came home to his workshop and garden. Thank God that, for the children, he was a warm and encouraging father.

"I don't know what rescued us all from that dreadful time in our lives. One day, I found myself thrusting my youngest child away as I prepared to lead my group. I knew something was terribly wrong.

"My little daughter's tears finally shocked me out of being possessed . . . brought me face to face with myself!"

There was silence as the women listening sensed the full danger in the woman's experience.

❖ ❖ ❖

The second woman waited, then began to speak:

"I carried all of the burdens during those painful years. Hardening my heart for so long let something else slip in the door. I can see it in the photographs taken of me during that time, the set of my jaw, the tilt of my head. My face became tough and cold.

"When I look back, at myself, it is with a deep compassion. I needed to have that toughness, then, but also to let it go. How impatient that harder side of me was with my womanly needs and hurt! I could not face the pain underneath or minister to it myself.

"Saddest of all was the loneliness. Women friends were driven away by my competitiveness, except for a very few who were as possessed as I. But I could not bear their cutoffness from feelings any more than they could bear mine. One by one, they all left.

"Isolated and alone, I spent those terrible years hating men, most women, and, of course, myself. What finally broke the alienation was being held by a warm, silent man who refused to be drawn into words . . . simply held me closely until I started to cry. As my weeping deepened into sobs, I began to return to myself."

The three women sat in silence to honour the woman's words, then parted quietly to prepare a cup of tea.

❖ ❖ ❖

When the women came together again, they gathered close around the fire. The third woman began to speak:

"I was touched as you spoke of being silently held and return-ing to yourself. My experience was quite different. I was full of anger at my husband. He had said something that hurt me, and I held it to my heart.

"What could have been useful anger, if I had communicated it, became an entrenched rage. The insult became precious and exaggerated as I nursed my grievances and refused my husband's apologies. I shut myself into my study.

"I can see, now, the Masculine posturing in what I did, and how it cut me off from my husband's caring and honest concern. Even as my husband apologized, my animus convinced me that I was right, and I shoved my husband away. If only I had been able to let the flesh-and-blood man reach me, the inner imposter might have been ex-posed.

"One morning, I realized that I couldn't stop being nasty to my husband. I felt as miserable as he. Yet, I was caught in something per-verse that wouldn't let loose of either of us.

"Late that afternoon, a woman friend came by and took me briefly aside. She spoke with me so caringly and seemed to see my pain. Rather than drawing me into words, she simply reached out her hand and stroked my aching head. She must have known how desperately I had needed to cry, for I sobbed a long while after she wrapped my shoulders warmly in her sweater.

"She asked if I would come with her the next day for the mineral baths and massage that our town is known for, then spoke a few words to my husband that, somehow, he understood.

"In the few days after that, she came back several times. Together we scrubbed with a bucket of hot suds . . . the whole house, the walls, the floors.

"Then, as the last rays of the late afternoon sun bathed the room, we washed the windows in my study."

The wind blows lightly
             . . . leaves drift down.

Her possession

How might it have been different for you, when you were terribly upset and full of harsh self-judgement, if there had been a place where you could be received by a woman whom you trusted?

If the woman had listened in silence as you began to speak? And there had been a feeling of such simple acceptance from her that you were able to weep . . . finally, able to weep out all of the confusion and pain that you had held inside for so long . . .

And she wordlessly held your hand.

How might your life be different?

Her individuation

> I sit listening . . .
>   The wind blows
>   a woman's image to me.

Although the schedule had been pressing, I felt quite satisfied at a recent decision to take more time for myself . . . one-half hour a day, for walking or reflection.

Then, that night, I awoke and was transfixed by moonlight streaming in at the window . . . and at the image of a woman . . . scrawny and malnourished . . . her face covered with ashes . . . clothing torn by thorns.

"I am the neglected and crazy part of you . . . the holy part inside, which you so often deny . . . bustling between kitchen and studio, cheerful and productive.

> "Don't you see I am dying?
>   When will you recognize me
>   as the most precious part of yourself?
>   When will you grant me sovereignty?
>   When will you give me your soul?"

> I knelt and wept in the moonlight . . .
>   . . . let my tears wash the ashes from her face.

The years pass. A woman matures. Her work with her Masculine side ripens . . . her contributions to the society around her carefully brought to harvest. The Self calls insistently. She must finally hear and respond . . . or take the other path of hardening her heart against the voice within calling her to become herself.

A woman must be very clear, now, in her ongoing task. As she negotiates the voyage from the societal towards the Self, her entire experience is transformed. She can begin to reject the inner patriarchal decrees from the past that judged her so mercilessly . . . that made her see her own anguish as simply another indication of her inadequacy and shame.

With this transformation, a woman can accept feelings inside herself that were forbidden to her before. She can accept, newly, her failures, her lacks, her obsessions . . . even her occasional craziness . . . as she holds in her awareness all the ways she has suffered in striving to fulfill values that were not her own.

At last a woman cradles in her arms the woundedness of being herself. No longer casting it out as the impediment that prevents her growth, she can embrace her woundedness as the essence, the soul of her uniqueness . . . that which has enabled her to become herself.

With this final acceptance of her woundedness, a woman's perception of her own suffering undergoes a profound healing. What had been the source of greatest shame, that most loathed in herself, slowly reveals itself to her as the seed of her truest gift . . . her pearl of greatest price, grown from her gravest flaw. She is released into her wholeness.

Finally, as a woman matures, she gives up the expectation of reaching a point of bare adequacy and moving on from there. At last, she understands that her task is simply to accept her woundedness . . . and to walk ahead with courage and compassion . . . keeping faith with her own life.

This is her individuation.

❖ ❖ ❖

A woman sat alone and considered her condition. She was an editor of scientific journals who had recovered from starvation in all aspects of her life:

"I began to feel the poignancy of my own wounding . . . the poignancy of those old patterns set up, so long ago, as a protection against further wounding, in my little child way.

"I said, once, to my counsellor many months ago, 'But my patterns are pathological,' and she replied, 'Then that is finally what makes all the going back into one's personal history worthwhile. To be able to see the original wounding with such pathos, that you at last can feel compassion for that terribly wounded little child who wanted so strongly to survive that she was willing to adopt extreme patterns.'

"From the moment I heard those words, I knew that I must trust that my uniqueness stemmed from my own kind of wounding . . . grew directly out of it, not divorced or split off from it. I knew, from that day forward, that one day I would be able to stop loathing my woundedness . . . and hold it in esteem."

A second woman spoke:

"My parents must have wanted a completely different child! If my talents could not win instant fame, I was scorned for even trying. I couldn't imagine taking the risk of becoming more myself. All I had ever experienced was humiliation and despair for revealing, in any way, who I really was.

"My animus reflected my parents' negating attitude. Years ago, I named my inner judges 'the shit boys.' Far from being supportive helpers in my efforts to develop, they were the eternal critics who scorned anything I brought forth from within myself.

"I learned quite skillfully, over the years, to use myself as mirror and mentor for the creativity of others. I have helped many wordless people express themselves in poems . . . helped those with no sense of identity tell the pathos of their lives in writing their autobiographies. I have watched the radiance of dance emerge from eighty- and ninety-year-old bodies as our troupe toured the countryside working with the elderly.

"I have had to realize, as my deepest truth, that I could help bring out their spirit, while mine was held captive within.

"I wish, now, to be present to what is real inside me, to the anguish and chaos and fear. No longer to dress it up in impeccable tutorial service to the gifts of others . . . further and further estranged from myself . . . feeding on anything to fill the hollow.

"There are poems unborn inside me, and, if I live long enough, I wish to bring them to birth. I wish to stand firm against the expectations of disgrace for daring to have something inside me of my very own.

"Most of all, I wish to stay close to the apprehension of being immediately shamed. For if I only rise above my fear, as I have so often done, there will be no one to witness my wretchedness and mortification . . . no one to attend my wounding . . . no one to allow it to begin its process of transformation and healing.

Her individuation

"I have finally acknowledged my wounding as the thing in all the world that is most truly mine . . . and that acknowledgement has allowed me to begin to be myself.

"I am able, at last, to witness my wounding
                              . . . and I am, at last, in peace."

The sky darkens towards the evening.

How might your life have been different if, once as you sat in the darkness, suffering the most piercing shame for simply being yourself . . . you had sensed a presence nearby, sitting quietly in the shadows attending you . . . a forgiving Feminine presence?

If you had felt such a flow of compassion from that ancient presence . . . that you could begin to accept your flaws, even your gravest faults? And, deeply comforted in the flow of that compassion . . . you were able, at last, to embrace your own woundedness . . .

How might your life be different?

Her return

> *I sit listening . . .*
>   *the wind blows*
>   *a woman's image to me:*

> *"I have crossed a chasm . . . stand alone, now, in a chamber . . . carved of dark, rich crystals, glowing deep within the earth.*

> *A distant call beckons me onward . . . to a still more glowing chamber . . . then to another, richer still . . . chamber opening unto chamber, each glows more darkly than the last.*

> *I know that these are the chambers of a mansion that once belonged to my Mother . . .*

> *And I know that the openings . . .*
>   *chamber unto chamber . . .*
>   *are the moments of my life."*

Out of a woman's acceptance of her woundedness comes a quietness and sense of peace. The transformation of the Masculine energy within her, from negating to supporting, allows her to become herself. She redirects her efforts from the outer to the inner realm . . . finally makes the return to Archetypal Feminine ground with her roots in the guiding principles of the deeper Self.

❖ ❖ ❖

A woman speaks:

"I feel as if I am becoming who I was meant to be. After all the years of outer-directed energy, I am coming home to the Feminine . . . coming home to myself. I am allowing myself to become a mature woman in the truest and deepest sense.

"Sometimes, as I sit listening quietly within, it seems as if the very air in the house has been transformed. There is a hush of tranquillity, an attitude of devotion filling every room.

"I feel a sense of connection to the self that I have been at other times in my life . . . to the girl and maiden from the past, to the developed woman of adulthood . . . and to the older woman I know that I shall someday be.

"As I allow myself to mature, a clarity emerges, never there before. I seem to know more surely than I have ever known what is mine to do, what must be left undone. There is a growing strength within me . . . and I realize, that while life's difficulties do not disappear, my steadfastness holds firm.

"As I allow myself to mature, an awareness comes of a slender ribbon of energy, no longer robust, as in my youth. I learn to tend it carefully . . . avoid excess, exercise restraint. To use my strength ever more sacramentally, for I suffer more each time I use it in service to old distractions.

"As I allow myself to mature, I find that I must do things the old, slow ways . . . perform my work so quietly that some part of me can always be listening . . . listening for the deeper sense of my life. Those few brief moments each day, that 'closet' in time that, as a young woman, I set aside to listen, are no longer enough for me.

Her return

"What I could slip by with while I was still in service to the values of the society around me is likely to make me ill now, at the level of the Self. I sense that the greater quantity of my time is being required, now, to reflect at the window seat . . . to see the leaves drift down . . . watch the snow clouds gather.

"As I allow myself to mature, I see that if I depart from my center and am over-busy for too long, it may take many days of quietness for me to make the return. And in dry periods, when the Self seems not to be present, I know that my task is simply to wait. Now, the only task . . . in devotion and submission . . . is to wait upon the Self."

❖ ❖ ❖

Slowly over the years, as a woman allows herself to mature, she sees that she must keep the physical realm so simple that each object in her household becomes translucent . . . revealing its meaning and spirit to her as she polishes it in her hands . . . that this is her testament of devotion, the loving redirection of her energy from outer to inner realm . . . and the holding and hallowing in her hands of the moments of life itself.

Alone on the barren rocks,
I listen to the wind . . .
It blows the ancient, raucous call
of distant wild geese.
I know I am coming home.

How might your life have been different if, through the years, you had felt that there would finally be time enough for you?

If, very early one morning . . . as you sat at the window seat and watched a silvery mist slowly rise from the meadow . . . you heard, far off in the distance, the call of the wild geese?

And you remembered the first time you had heard that cry, many years before . . . with a chill up the back of your neck. And that you had known, even then, that the haunting, primordial cry . . . was the call of the ancient Feminine returning.

How might your life be different?

Her legacy

I sit listening . . .
the wind blows
a child's song to me . . .

An old woman sits in the dusk, an unlighted candle on the table before her. She picks up a soft cloth, begins to polish the small statue in her hands, as she has done many times before. She polishes the statue of a woman . . . keeping vigil in the stillness . . . polishing her own sense of life.

She hums a children's song that she says is very old . . . then she begins to sing:

" *'This is the way we sow our seed . . .*
gather our grain . . .
bake our bread . . .
This is the way we tend our lives
so early in the morning.'

"*I learned that song, and others like it, at an afternoon gathering for children and their mothers, many years ago. Songs that told of the ways of woman, long before I was born . . . still knowing that the spirit with which a task was fulfilled made a difference in the greater order . . . and let a rhythm and meaning emerge from every step of her work.*

"*Woman, long ago, still in touch with the mysteries of nature . . . singing to the grass and the wind . . . knowing that her song was heard. Pouring out her devotion, as she poured out her menstrual blood, back to the earth again.*"

The old woman sighs:

"*Ah, those young mothers, that afternoon, had lost touch with so much of that. I cannot forget their faces, so desperate and stricken, as they sang their choruses of the ancient circle dances there in the meadow with their children . . . cut off from any meaning that might have made their tasks alive.*

"*That generation of woman . . . cut off from roots in the earth . . . or from knowing how to replenish the earth with their own womanly flow. So much of their Feminine energies blocked within them, like their milk, in those decades when women heeded the advice to schedule and bottle-feed their young.*

"*I sang a lament, that afternoon in the meadow, that a patriarchal way so pervaded . . . that woman no longer trusted her own instincts to nourish herself and her young.*

"*I sang a lament that women no longer encouraged an opening unto each moment that could allow it to unfold to the next . . . that they no longer let their own lives be alive and teach them how to live.*

"*I sang a lament that afternoon that the old ways of tending nature were dying. For I feared that, as they died, the life in our souls would die, too.*

"*I sang a lament, that afternoon in the meadow, for women of every age, overburdened and overworked, pressed between efforts for those they loved and the weight of their work in the world . . . with no time for rest or reflection on what their life was about.*"

Her legacy

The old woman pushes a strand of hair from her face:

"Ah, that was so long ago . . . so many ways were lost. I learned the songs as well as I could, so that someone might keep them alive.

"Once, as our circle of women came together a few years ago, I wakened, restless in the night . . . unable to go back to sleep. I sat for a long time on the terrace, wrapped in a woolen robe . . . watching the moon shine down on the wind-bared trees below.

"When I finally came back to the cottage, there was a glimmer of light from the kitchen. My old friend sat there, alone, by candle-light, the only one in the circle older than I. It was she who had taught the songs on the meadow that afternoon, long ago. She polished this little statue that night, telling me of her life . . . and mine.

"She left me her shawl when she died.

"She's gone now, but every year at this season, in the middle of the night, I sit, as she did, for so many years, polishing this statue . . . polishing, alone, while the younger women sleep."

The old woman puts down the statue, reaches for the matches to light the candle:

"That afternoon, long ago, I lamented. But as I sit polishing this statue, I know that a difference can be made as we women remember again to keep faith with our ancient ground . . . remember that the stillness at our center, as we sit in the glow of a candle, can help return a sense of order to the cosmos reflecting us.

"We lost touch for a little while, in the busyness of this world. But I know that a difference can be made if we women can remember that our blood and passion are needed . . . our fierce, tender love for the land. We can bring the cycles to wholeness again as we pour out our devotion . . . as we sing, once more, to the earth."

The old woman unfolds the shawl, wraps it around herself.

"We lost touch for a little while, in the noise and pain around us. But, I know that, for the children, a difference can be made if we can return to a sense of the ancient Maternal . . . return to the cradling embrace that offers solace and protection . . . that strengthens their sense of Self.

"We lost touch for a little while. But I know that, for the men around us, a difference can be made if we can remember a way of being that gives them a place to return, a Yin to receive their Yang warmth. A difference can be made as we help them learn to heal their own pain as well as ours . . . help them comfort their fears and affirm their heroic strivings."

The old woman smoothes the shawl . . . straightens her shoulders beneath it.

"The earth, the children, the men . . . they all need what was lost. But it is for our daughters . . . our daughters . . . that women must remember all that was left behind. It is our daughters who cannot go on with their lives unless we show them the way.

Her legacy

"It is for our daughters that we must rekindle the ancient ways of the Yin . . . help them hold the truth of their knowing deep within themselves and witness it with the full passion and power of their womanly being . . . help them to remember that the truth each woman holds within will come to realization not only through outer doing but through her inner holding.

"We lost touch for a little while, as we gained power over things seen . . . that woman's ancient chthonic power has to do with things unseen. For our daughters, we must return to the sacred Feminine ways of holding within our hearts our visions for their lives . . .

> *Of holding within,*
> > *the essence and splendor*
> > > *of our daughters' possibilities.*
> > > *. . . the possibilities of all women*
> > > > *. . . and dreaming them into being."*

The old woman quietly picks up the statue and bends her head low to her task. As the candle flickers out, she sits in the darkness . . .

> *. . . polishing*
> > *. . . polishing.*

How might your life have been different if, one morning in the earliest springtime, something had drawn you to the woods? And in the cool mist, you had seen women of all ages, from every epoch in history, waiting in the stillness.

And you had knelt among them . . . had heard the trembling in the voices of the older women as they spoke of preparation, of individual sacrifice . . . of woman offering, out of her own uniqueness, her suffering, her devotion. And if, as you listened, you had a glimmer of hope that your work to develop yourself might make a tiny difference . . . help heal an ancient Archetype . . . restore a longed-for balance in the greater cosmos.

And you felt a sense of wonder, knowing that each woman kneeling there was considering inside herself what her offering would be . . .

How might your life be different?

I sit listening

   as the wind

      asks its eternal questions:

      What will our generation of women

        pass on to our daughters?

         What will be our legacy

        to the daughters

          of our great-granddaughters?

And the earth

whispers her response:

Know yourself . . .

. . . yourself.

The Author

Judith Duerk

Born in the Midwest of a family with strong religious ties, Judith Duerk followed the call of her early love for music. She earned B.S. and M.S. degrees from The Juilliard School, studied as a postgraduate at the Mozarteum in Salzburg and at Indiana University, and taught music at the university level before beginning preparatory work in the fields of psychotherapy and music therapy.

For many years, she has led groups of women on Retreat. She says, *"I am awed by the depth of healing that comes as women sit in a circle, by the power of women keeping silence together, and by the truth in their sharing."* In addition to her daily work as therapist, she teaches T'ai Chi Ch'uan and works with the ancient Taoist healing art of Chi Kung.

Judith notes that the sensitivity and spiritual strength of the men around her have been helpful role models for her animus. Her two sons are grown. She recalls that *"when they were younger, they liked to joke that all their mother cared about was Yin-Yang-Jung . . . but they really knew better."*

Her husband is a woodsman and artisan. Their lives together have been deeply nurtured by the greater cycles of nature, and they seek to know how to nurture those cycles in return.

Deepening your Circle

Ideas to help draw your circle of women together:

Over the last ten years, in hundreds of women's circles around the country, women have gathered to study Judith Duerk's books. In a typical evening, one woman may read a single chapter aloud while the others sit listening, with their eyes closed. And then at the end, they may share their personal experiences or images—or perhaps memories from old dreams—that are evoked during the reading.

Your circle may want to reflect on the ending questions for each chapter, *"How might your life have been different if . . .?"* You may want to expand your reflection with the discussion questions offered here.

You may want to begin your circle the way Judith often begins her retreats: She asks the women to imagine that they are inviting the important women from their lives to join them, to sit just slightly behind them in the circle, all of the women from their whole life . . . those who were supportive and affirming, and perhaps those who might have been, but weren't . . . "the special woman teacher who reached out to you in second grade, the favorite auntie who always made you the lemon crisp cookies, the kindly neighbor lady who plucked the red tulip and gave it to you over the fence . . . and the woman professor or mentor who taught you so much." Consider your relationship with each of these women, positive and negative. Let them all be there surrounding you in your gathering of women.

Reading Group Suggestions
for *I SIT LISTENING TO THE WIND*

HER GROUNDING IN THE FEMININE

A sense of time (pages 20-25)

"For under the pressures of modern life, time has become compressed" (pages 23). How do you experience the compression of time? How might your life be different if you knew there would finally be enough time for *you*? Pages 21-22 describe "a shift in the experiencing of time." Has this kind of shift ever happened to you? What were your thoughts and feelings about this?

A sense of identity (pages 26-30)

The woman musician in this chapter "knew truly who she was and the value of what she gave . . . she did not make herself give more" (page 28). What are the signs that signal to you that a woman knows herself? What women mentors in your life seem to know who they truly are? What are some things you do or could do to recognize your own identity and worth?

A sense of sustenance (pages 31-36)

This chapter describes the choice between a "wire" mother and a "soft" mother. What is your experience of each? How might your life be different if you had a place among women where you knew you could always go for safety and comfort?

A *sense of voice* (pages 37-42)

Each woman in this chapter describes finding a way to speak in her own voice, to express herself in her own style. Think of a time when you felt no one understood you. How did you feel when you were unable to communicate what you knew you wanted to say? How might it have been different for you if supportive women had listened to you and encouraged you to let your true voice emerge?

A *sense of sacredness* (pages 43-47)

In this chapter Judith describes small, silken bags that each woman symbolically fills with something that is sacred to her. What container would you chose? As you picture this container, think of some fact, memory, or image from your life that you would like to place in its empty space. What feelings surface for you as you picture doing this?

HER WORK WITH THE MASCULINE WITHIN HER

Welcoming her energy (pages 52-58)

In this chapter, the women teachers speak about their experience of first meeting their animus/masculine energy. What are your memories of first meeting this energy within yourself? Do you remember "strife" between you and your mother at this time? Did *anybody* help you to welcome this energy in yourself? How would you like to help your daughter or niece welcome this energy in herself?

Embracing her encounter (pages 59-63)

"Slowly over the years, a woman's awareness of herself deepens as, again and again, she encounters the Masculine within" (page 62). What is your experience over the years of confronting your own inner masculine side? How has your relationship with this masculine energy changed over time? How have you been able to call upon its strengths rather than its judgement?

Bringing forth her feeling values (pages 64-70)

Five women in this chapter share their experiences of feeling cut off from themselves, from their creativity, from their feelings. What do you recognize in their stories that relates to you? How have you experienced this kind of pain? How might it be different for you if there were a place where you could go whenever you felt overwhelmed by your feelings?

Honouring her intuition (pages 71-76)

Judith writes that the intuition of woman is very hard to describe. How does your own intuition work? What does it do for you? Is it ever troublesome? What gifts does your intuition bring you?

Distinguishing her life (pages 77-81)

The woman in this chapter speaks of two different meanings for distinguishing her life: One is the more common definition of "earning honours," while the other is finding the meaning of one's individual life. In what ways have you seen your women friends or women leaders distinguish their lives in each of these ways? What are your own experiences of these different types of "distinguishing"?

HER RETURN TO FEMININE GROUND

Her contagion (pages 86-92)

This chapter describes the eruption of misunderstanding and ill will between women brought about by an "untamed animus." What is your own experience of this happening between women? How have you and the women around you been able to recover from this kind of competition or conflict? What do you find helps you keep from trying to "out-woman" other women?

Her possession (pages 93-98)

Possession by the animus is more gripping and lasts a good deal longer than the kind of contagion described in the previous chapter. It is much harder to break its hold. Have you ever had an experience like this or seen it with a woman friend or relative? In what ways did you, or the woman, become "swallowed up" by the episode, convinced that you were "right"? How might it have been different for you if there had been someplace where you could safely weep out all of the confusion and pain?

Her individuation (pages 99-105)

In this chapter Judith speaks of woundedness as an intrinsic and precious part of woman's individuation process. Were you surprised to read this? What is your understanding of this? Your experience of this?

Her return (pages 106-109)

This chapter ends with an image of wild geese as a symbol of the Feminine, with a woman responding to the wildness of their call. "After all the years of outer-directed energy, I am coming home to the Feminine . . . coming home to myself" (page 109). What image holds the symbol of the Feminine for you? What is your experience of "coming home"?

Her legacy (pages 110-115)

In this concluding chapter Judith describes the legacy women leave for each other. What legacy have you received from women of the past? From women in your family? From women who have influenced you in other areas of your life? How has their presence in your life made a difference? What is the legacy that you are leaving to your own daughters or nieces, to all women of the future?

❖ ❖ ❖

At the end of each section of this book, there is a two-page poem in which the earth murmurs, sings, and whispers her response. What is *your* response?

Innisfree Classics that
Call to the Deep Heart's Core

BELOVED BEST-SELLERS
BY JUDITH DUERK
Circle of Stones
Woman's Journey to Herself
I Sit Listening to the Wind
Woman's Encounter Within Herself

BEAUTIFUL EXPLORATIONS OF THE
FEMININE SIDE OF GOD BY JOYCE RUPP
The Star in My Heart
Experiencing Sophia, Inner Wisdom
Prayers to Sophia
A Companion to The Star in My Heart

A COMPLETE
WORKSHOP IN A BOOK
**A Woman's Book of
Money & Spiritual
Vision**
*Putting Your
Financial Values into
Spiritual Perspective*
by Rosemary Williams

A BOOK TO
REMIND US
WHAT FOOD IS FOR
The Tao of Eating
*Feeding Your Soul
through Everyday
Experiences with Food*
by Linda R. Harper
Foreword by Thomas Moore

A BOOK TO READ
IF YOU ARE TOO
BUSY TO READ
Sabbath Sense
*A Spiritual Antidote
for the Overworked*
by Donna Schaper

NEW INSPIRATION
FROM A WOMAN'S
CLASSIC
Return to the Sea
*Reflections on
"Gift from the Sea"
by Anne
Morrow Lindbergh*
by Anne Johnson
Foreword by Reeve Lindbergh

*Call for Our Free Catalog
1-800-367-5872.*

*Find Innisfree books
in your local bookstore.*

*Visit our website at
www.InnisfreePress.com.*